Bible Names and Genealogy: Volume One

Pentateuch - History - Books of Poetry - Major Prophets - Minor Prophets

The Pentateuch View

Follow the ★ for the blood line of Jesus

Copyright © 2019 Timothy McCullough

ISBN 9781645507222

All rights reserved. No part of this book may be used or reproduced by any means, graphic, electronic, or mechanical, including photocopying, recording, taping or by any information storage retrieval system without the written permission of the publisher except in the case of brief quotations embodied in critical articles and reviews.

Because of the dynamic nature of the Internet, any web addresses or links contained in this book may have changed since publication and may no longer be valid. The views expressed in this work are solely those of the author and do not necessarily reflect the views of the publisher, and the publisher hereby disclaims any responsibility for them.

Any people depicted in stock imagery provided by Thinkstock are models, and such images are being used for illustrative purposes only.

Matchstick Literary
1-888-306-8885
www.matchliterary.com
orders@matchliterary.com

Pentateuch

First five books of Old Testament. The word comes from the Greek words Penta "five". In the Hebrew Bible, the first five books are called the Torah, law or teaching.

Genesis

Exodus

Leviticus

Numbers

Deuteronomy

Table of Contents

1. Introduction
2. Guide
3. Adam and Eve
4. Japhath
5. Canaan
6. Shem
7. Peleg
8. Abraham
9. Genesis 14 - Valley of Siddim
11. Isaac
12. Genesis 36 - Basemath
13. The land of Seir
14. Kings that reigned in the land of Edom
15. Jacob
16. Reuben - Simeon - Levy
17. Judah - Issachar - Zebulun
18. Gad - Asher - Joseph
19. Benjamin - Dan - Naphtali
20. Women who saved the male children
21. Kohath
22. God given talents
23. Numbers Ch1 - (The men) Concerning war
27. The "House of Levi"
28. 70 men of Israel
29. Concerning spying
31. Sons of Anak (The giants)
32. The faltered opposition against Moses and Aaron
33. Israel's exodus from Egypt
34. The "Tabernacle of Congregation"
35. 20 years old and upward ready for war
48. Numbers Ch 25 and Ch 31 – Israel's success
49. Kingdoms taken by Moses and divided
50. Dividing the land by inheritance
51. The giants of times past
52. Deuteronomy Ch 6-20
53. Deuteronomy Ch 21-34
54. Intro to the "Time Chart"
55. Helpful instructions to use the chart
56. Full chart according to Adam's creation and life
63. Number 666
64. Checking numbers
65. Index

Introduction

This book is a joy, indeed, to publish. The Bible is fascinating and is awesome. That is true "word" wise as well as numerically. It seems that numbers tend to indicate when God is, and has been in operation. The time line according to Adam's creation and death is in a form of a chart towards the end of this book. It is entirely based on the numbers that the Bible gives and from our study of the Pentateuch, the first five books of the Bible.

I have been impressed with a lot commentary that I have come across concerning the Bible. I have been surprised also concerning information that I have observed that is simply not in agreement it. This book is the result of reading and studying the Bible for myself, and the information here is based on facts according to it. The purpose of this book is to list every Bible name mentioned in the Pentateuch, leave them in order according to their place, position and/or birth in the story. This simply aids in comprehension when studying.

One of the amazing things about the Bible is that it speaks for itself concerning proclamations that were presented in the past for past futures, as well as the present day and the future from here. It is clear to me that it is good to read the Bible using your common sense. It should not be demonized, common sense that is. After all, the author is communicating the message through that of language. It takes a certain level of common sense to comprehend principal points of thought. God also, through his word, encourages us to place a priority on that of getting an understanding (Proverbs 4:7). One thing that we all should be mindful of is that God is the master of communication. He is capable of talking and responding to you on your level. So when we lack comprehension and spiritual insight, it's ok. It's ok because when you have a hungry heart for clarity concerning God's word you can get understand if you do at least four things: communicate to God that you have a desire for comprehensibility, admit you don't have it when you don't, don't pretend like you have it when you don't, and ask him for it. And also, know that he spiritually, may or may not reveal it to you at this time. And, as far as communication is concerned, let me add this. When speaking to him, one should not have the thought pattern that God is a robot; responding the same programmed way in all similar situations. Yet, at the same time, he does say that he was the same yesterday, today and forevermore. That is referring to who he is and what he stands for. What he called wrong years ago is still wrong today. Yet again, how he executes rewards and judgment may differ. He could be merciful to a wrong when a person repents or allow harsh consequences. In both cases, because of repentance, forgiveness can be gained. He is God, and it would only do us good to understand that. It would do us good also to understand that this is his program, his ship, or more appropriately, his world. And we should recognize that. From Adam on, ever man and woman should try to find out how they can walk and endeavor to be an asset to his plan. It would only be beneficial and would please him.

When reading his word, it is okay to say, "I don't understand that" or "Why would God do that?" But, also be willing to seek the word that he gave you for the answer. It is a conviction of mine when I say, it is important to be prayerful when reading God's word. Yes, although it is true that we should use common sense, which is a gift from God, it is from his spirit that we are enlightened to a deeper understanding.

Concerning this book, understanding the names of fathers, sons, daughters and wives is one part of getting an understanding of the picture that God himself paints. Understanding their roles also and the meaning of their names goes along with that. If you want a better understanding of that picture, then study. I would suggest on an early Saturday morning when it's quiet, and your calendar is clear, find a good spot. Have paper and pencil/pen and your Bibles (different versions). Start from Genesis 1:1 and don't skip over any verses. Write down ever name and number and prepare to be at it for the next couple of years. There will not be any reason to rush. Just enjoy yourself as your mind begins to absorb information from God. If you are like me, you will hear the flapping of the tents in the wind, and see the grass gently moving as the sheep are drinking water. You will be an invisible present, listening to Biblical conversations while waiting for the next event. What is good is that you will start from the beginning with a study mentality, as opposed to a "one year read through". You will have the foundation of the story for yourself. This book is a result of just that. I could add a little more each time I go back and reread, but this book would take longer to get published. As the name of this book suggests, all names are only from the Pentateuch. The Pentateuch consists of the first five books of the Bible in the Old Testament; Genesis, Exodus, Leviticus, Numbers and Deuteronomy. These are the books considered to be written by Moses. Again, this book contains just the names and genealogy given according to the Pentateuch. No changes, just what the, mostly referred to, King James version Bible makes clear. Although there are some opinions offered by the author, it is clear when that is the case. The Biblical information stands on its own.

In the book of Joshua, the "Book of Jasher" is mentioned". So I researched it and came across two different takes on what was considered to be the real "Book of Jasher" and have concluded that there is one, a "Book of Jasher" that is, but not one for viewing by you and me. More than likely, you would not feel assured that it is authentic. One copy was produced by a publishing company out of Utah. And let me tell you, it is good reading. I just did not have the conviction that the words were that of the real Book of Jasher mention in the Bible. The temptation to add the names given according to that book was overwhelming. But, the need for certainty was higher. I found more peace, not including those names as oppose to adding them. Enjoy.

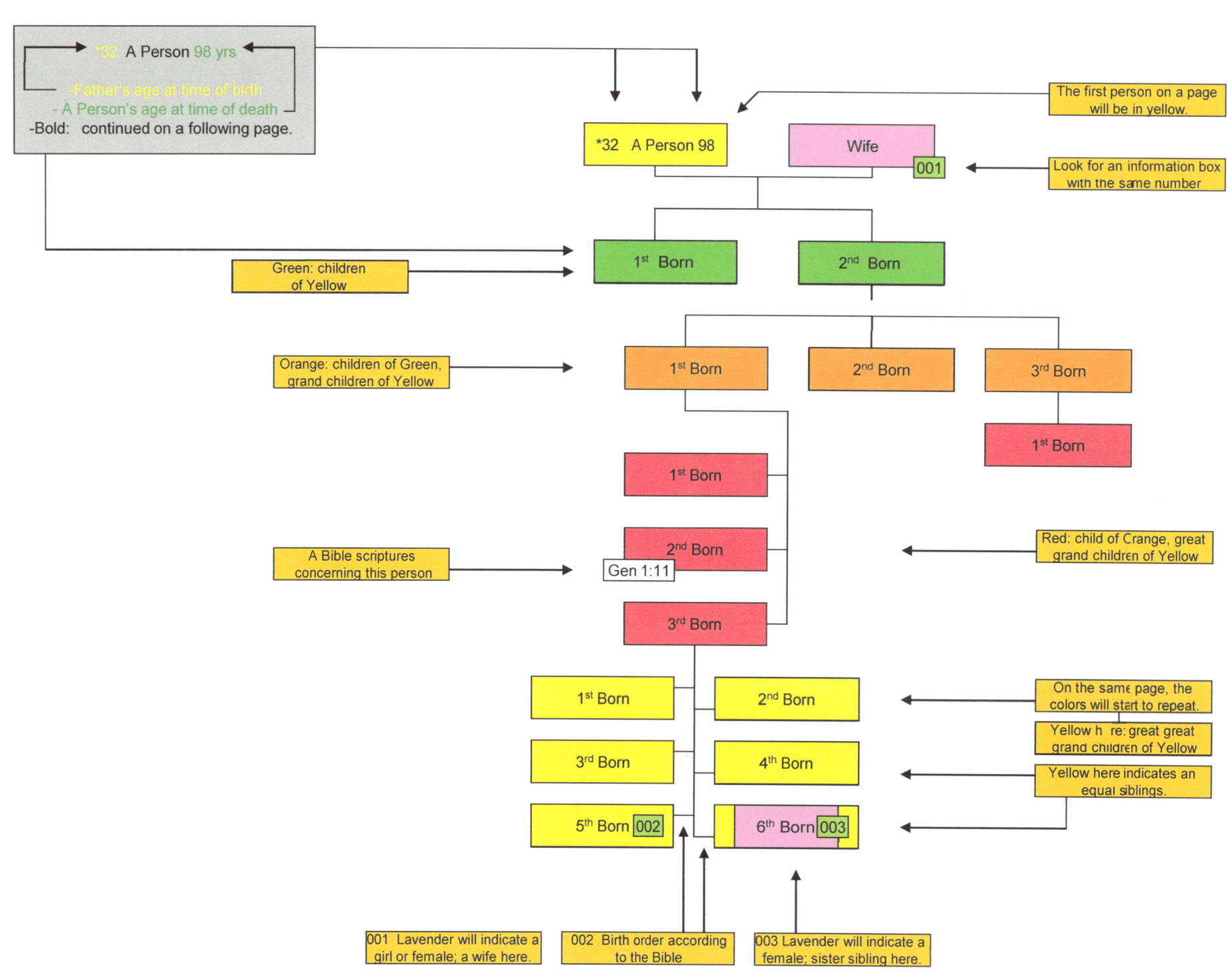

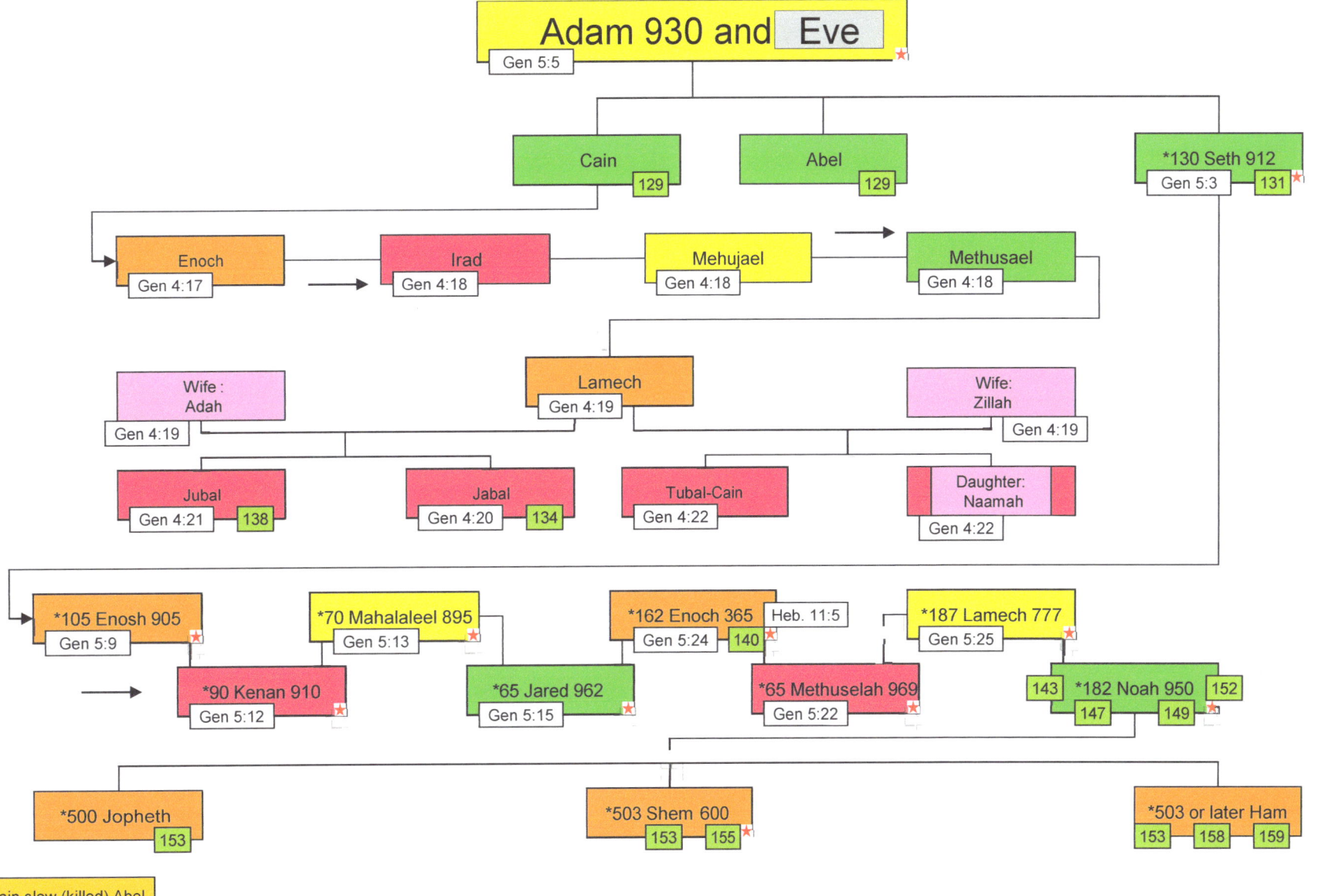

Japheth

*500 Japheth — Gen 5:22 | Gen 10:1 | Gen 6:10

Children of Japheth (Gen 10:2):
- **Gomer** (Gen 10:3)
- **Magog**
- **Madai**
- **Javan** (Gen 10:4)
- **Tubal**
- **Mashech**
- **Tiras**

Sons of Gomer (Gen 10:3):
- **Ashkenaz**
- **Riphath**
- **Togarmah**

Sons of Javan (Gen 10:4):
- **Elishan**
- **Tarshish**
- **Kittim**
- **Dodanim**

Ham

*503 (or later) Ham — Gen 10:1

Sons of Ham:
- **Cush** (Gen 10:6)
- **Mizraim** (Gen 10:13)
- **Phut** (Gen 10:6)
- **Canaan** (Gen 9:18) — [162] [165] [169] [171]

Sons of Cush (Gen 10:7):
- Seba
- Sabtah
- Nimrod (Gen 10:8) — [160]
- Havilah
- Raamah
- Subtecha

Children of Raamah:
- Sheba
- Dedan

Sons of Mizraim (Gen 10:13):
- Ludim
- Anamim
- Lehabim
- Naphtuhim (Gen 10:13)
- Pathrusim
- Casluhim (Gen 10:14)
- Caphtorim

---

160 He began to be a mighty one in the earth Gen 10:8-10. The beginning of his kingdom was Babel, Erech, Accad & Calnech in the land of Shinar. Out of that land went forth Assure, who is assumed to be the 2nd son of Shem and built Nineveh, Rehoboth, Calah and Resen. KJV

162 Canaan is the land of promise for God's people

165 The Canaanites were sexually sinful. Lev. 18:24

169 They performed human sacrifice. Lev. 20:2

171 God allows the sinful people to be overthrown.

Notable Point

God repented that he made man and it grieved him at his heart. He said he would destroy man, but Noah found grace in his site. (Gen 6:6-8) After the flood, God allows man to start again through Noah and his family.

Canaan
Gen 10:6

Sidon — 174, 178
Gen 10:19

Heth
Gen 10:15

Jebusite — 174

girgashite
I Chron 1

Arkite

Arvadites

Amorite — 182

Hivite
Gen 34:25 — 185

Sinite — 180

Zemazite
Gen 10:18

Hamathite
Gen 10:18

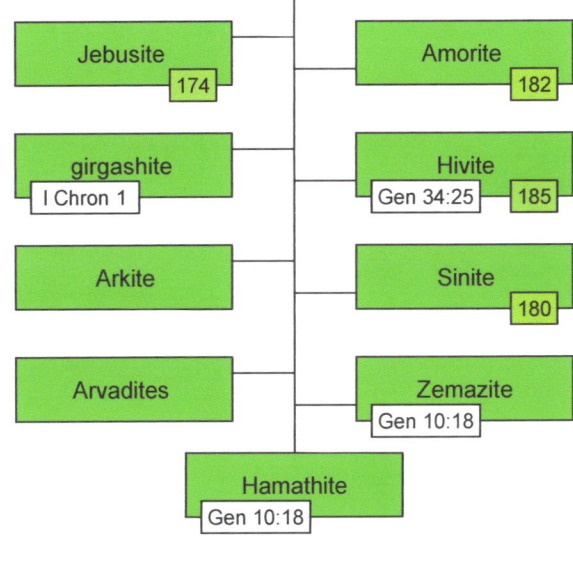

178 Today, Sidon is about 40 miles N. of Israel's border in the territory of Lebanon. It has been so, geographically, since the dividing of the land in Joshua's time. The distroyed city of Tyre, 20 miles south, is well Biblically noted also.

Canaan did begat the descendants of the different "ites": Jebus, Amor, Girga, Hiv, Ark, Sin, Aruad, Zema & Hamath.

174 The Bible clearly states the 1st and 2nd sons of Canaan Gen 10:15. It goes on to say that he also begat the "Ites" which namely states the tribal fathers. All of these descendants from Sidon to the Hamathite are considered "Canaanites".

180 The Sinites are said to have settled in the land down under which is Australia. They are also said to have settled in China depending on the documentary you read. Both could have some truth, although China seems more plausible. Where ever it is, Isaiah 49:12 called it the land of "Sinim". Was there ever a city built in honor and named after Canaan's son "Sin"?

185 In years to come from here, Shechem, a Hivite & son of a leader to be, Hamor, will sexually violate Dinah, daughter of Jacob & Leah who'll be new to the area, Gen. 34:2. This makes her brothers take revenge without Jacob's knowledge.

182 Mamre, Escho and Aner were all brothers and also Amorites who allied with Abram to rescue Lot when Lot was captured near Sodom and Gomorrah. Gen. 14:13, 14:22 Yet, the Amorites were sinful people. Gen 15:16. Some Amorites it seems, made choices that were not main stream.

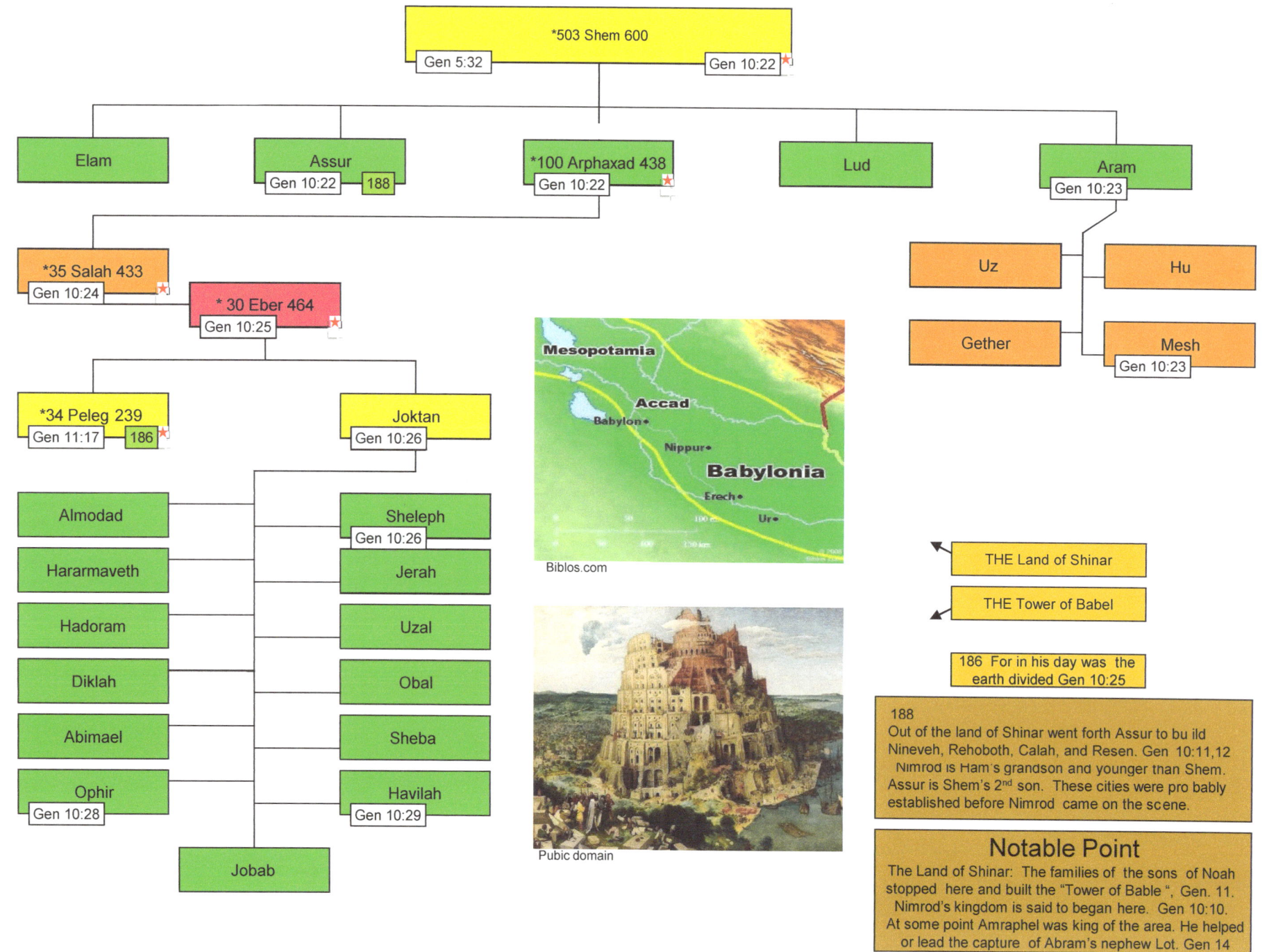

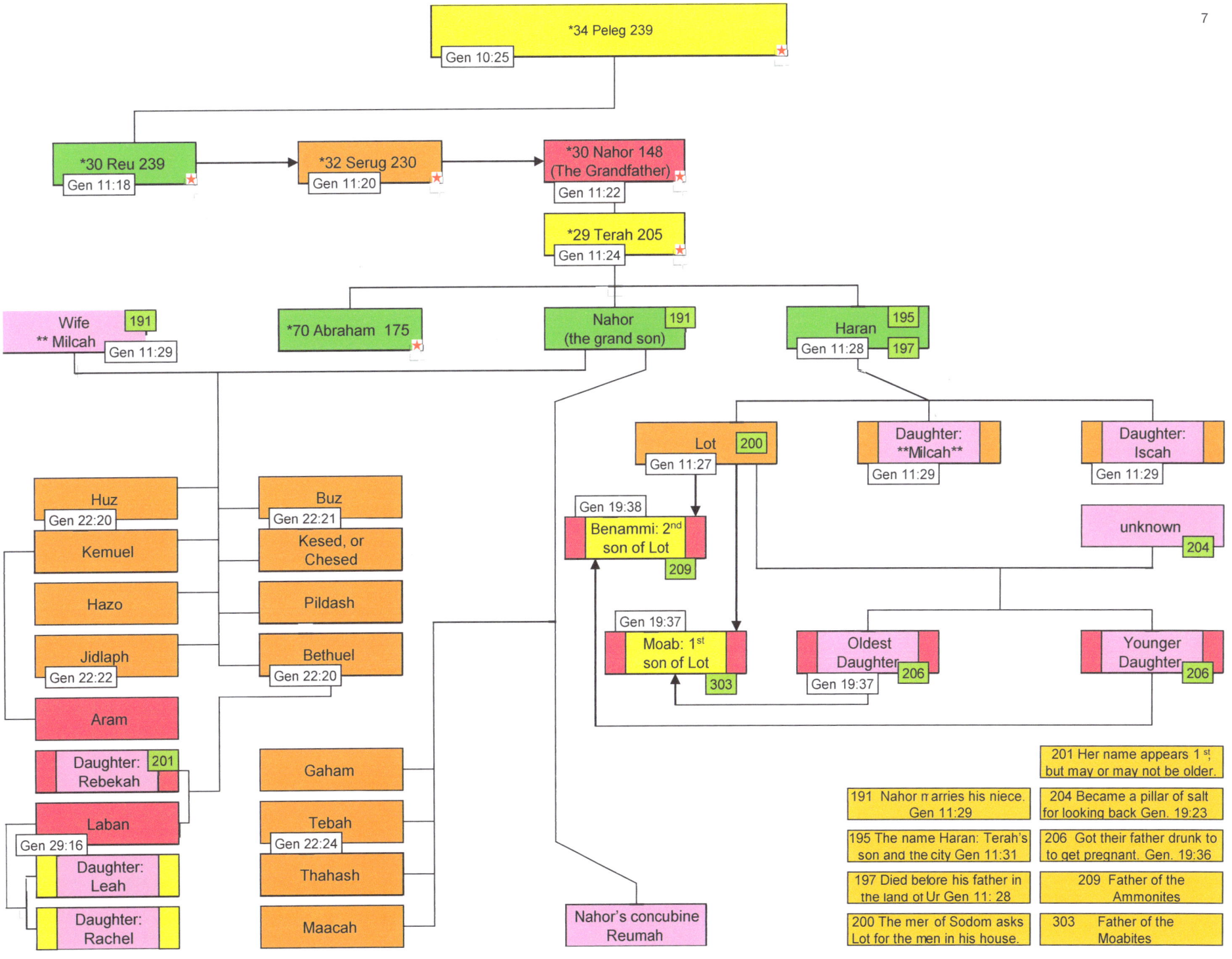

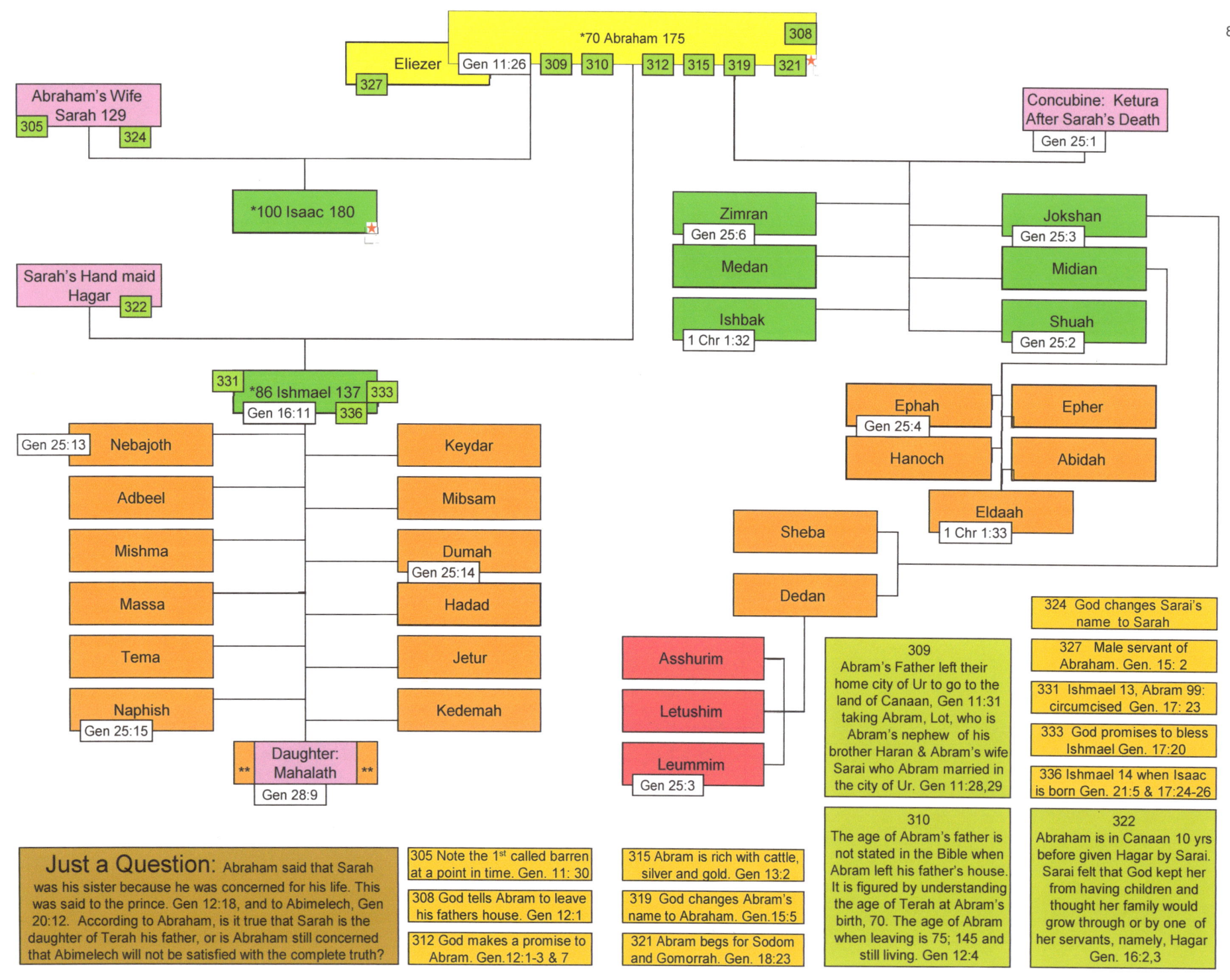

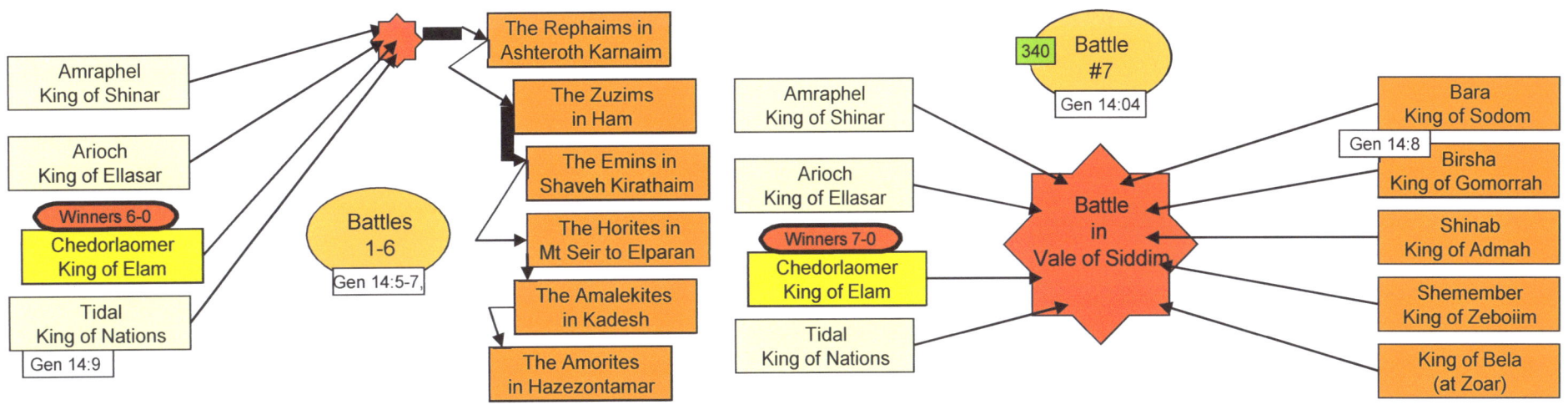

340 The joining of the Kings was prep for the war to come.	342 Abram meets the priest of the most high God.
345 Abram gives a tenth of everything Gen. 14:20	349 No additional information, before or after

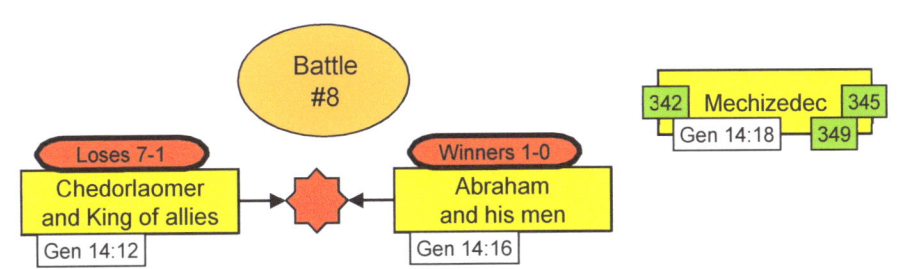

Gen 14:1-4 Explains a war of kings not mentioned up to this point in time. The sub-servant kings were subjected to Chedorlaomer for 12 years. In the 13th year, v4, these kings joined together in rebellion. After Chedorlaomer's conquests of near by areas, v5, 6, & 7 (battles 1-6) it appears that the rebellion of the 13th year turned into a manifestation of a physical battle a year or so later, in the "Vale of Siddim", KJV or "Valley of Siddim" AMP, Gen. 14:8. This was another victorious battle for king Chedodaomer who enjoyed the spoils of war. He also took captives into captivity...including Lot, Abram's nephew.

These particular battles are basically of no concern to Abram nor Lot. They are events that are "out of site-out of mind". Well, it would have been, if Lot had not been in the area. In all probability, Lot was not only <u>not targeted</u>, but was more than likely, not even known to exsist in the mind of king Chedorlaomer. Nevertheless, Lot is captured by this king. Lot also is the nephew of a man who has the promises of God with him. So when Abram heard that Lot was captured, he had one thing on his mind, to rescue his kin. In the process of that, he stopped king Chedodaomer's flow of victories. Gen. 14:14-16.

King Chedorlaomer is what you might call a "bad boy". Wrong or right, he fights hard and makes no apologies. When a person becomes a warrior and a ruthless individual on his level, it is kind of hard to hide them from history. There are sure to be some names that have fallen through the cracks throughout the ages that could have been elevated to the status of "unforgettable". However, opinion wise, king Chedorlaomer deserves his place in history. The Bible certainly takes note of him. Not for being a noble citizen, mind you. If someone studies war, regardless of which side is considered noble and which is considered the tyrant, you would have to study a character such as king Chedorlaomer. From the accounts of the Bible, this individual lived and breathed war. And, it surely appears that justice was not a motivator nor was it a friend. Outside looking in, king Chedorlaomer goes to war often, simply because he can. He is good at it and you would have to say, that he has the natural ability to command. It could be said that king Chedorlaomer has one of three choices in life. One, he could continue being the callous combatant figure that he is; two, choose to use his skills for the good of mankind, which he does not. Or three, he could simply make the choice to do something other than war altogether. Of course his response to the latter might be something

"If I cannot war and be on a conquest, then let me die."

Genesis 14:1 identifies king Chedorlaomer and his company of allies, four kings in all. Verse 2, identifies the king of Gomorra and the king of Sodom and their company of allies, five kings in all. Verses 3, identifies the location, which is the "Valley of Siddim". Verse 4, identifies the situation: the five kings of which the king of Gomorra is apart, served king Chedorlaomer for twelve years, who is the leader of the allied pack of four. Verses 4, goes on to say that in the thirteenth year, the five allied kings rebelled. This could mean that they rebelled in the 13th year and a war took place as a result, in the 13th year. But, there's another possibility that could be seen as more favorable. It could mean that they, in the 13th year, indeed rebelled, but against the rule of thumb, whatever that would incorporate, and would have a summit to plan and declared a formal resistance. This would stand for a war taking place in the, considerable, near future. If this is the case, then it would give a king Chedorlaomer time to put them on his schedule, as matters to deal with, resulting from the rebellion. This would then suggest that the five kings are not seen as an offensive, imminent threat.

Verses 5 and 6 do confirm that after the issue of the thirteenth year came to light, that in the fourteenth year, Chedorlaomer is occupied with the Rephaims, Zuzims, Emins, and the, "Horites in their own mount Seir". Then verse number 7 says, about king Chedorlaomer and his itinerary,

"And they returned, and came to Enmishpat, which is Kadesh, and smote all the country of the Amalekites, and also the Amorites, that dwelt in Hazezontamar. "

Now read verse number 8.

"And there went out the king of Sodom, and the king of Gomorrah, and the king of Admah, and the king of Zeboiim, and the king of Bela (the same is Zoar) and they joined battle with them in the vale of Siddim;"

Verse 7, says that after defeating the Amalekites, they (Chedorlaomer and his allies) defeated the Ammorites that dwelt in Hazezontamar. Verse 8, says, the same is Zoar. There, the five kings went out and joined in (engaged in) battle with Chedorlaomer. This is not Chedorlaomer place of residence. It is a place that he just so happened to be "working" that day and the five kings decided to catch up with him there, about a year and a half or so after the rebellion was openly declared. King Chedorlaomer defeated them also. It will take a man who has God on his side to stop him. And that is what Abraham did.

Abraham was born in the Adamic year of 1949 and was 75 years old when he left his father's house and went to Canaan. That was in the Adamic year 2024. It was in the Adamic year of 2034, ten years after living in Canaan, that Sarah gave Abraham her maid, in which Ishmael was born a year later, in the Adamic year of 2035. It is within this ten year period that the battle in the Valley of Siddim, is safely thought to have occurred.

Alexander the Great will be born in about one and half thousand years from this point in the year 356 BC. The similarities that he have with king Chedorlaomer are well noted. Both are extremely fearless. Both wore the position of being a commander and a warrior like a natural gloves. And both tired not after a conquest and have conquered consecutively, time and time again. Jewishvirtuallibrary.org states that Alexander the Great became a student of Aristotle, who spawn his great love for literature. If that is true and he loved literature. It would not be hard to imagine that Alexander the Great read about the king and got inspired even to a greater height.

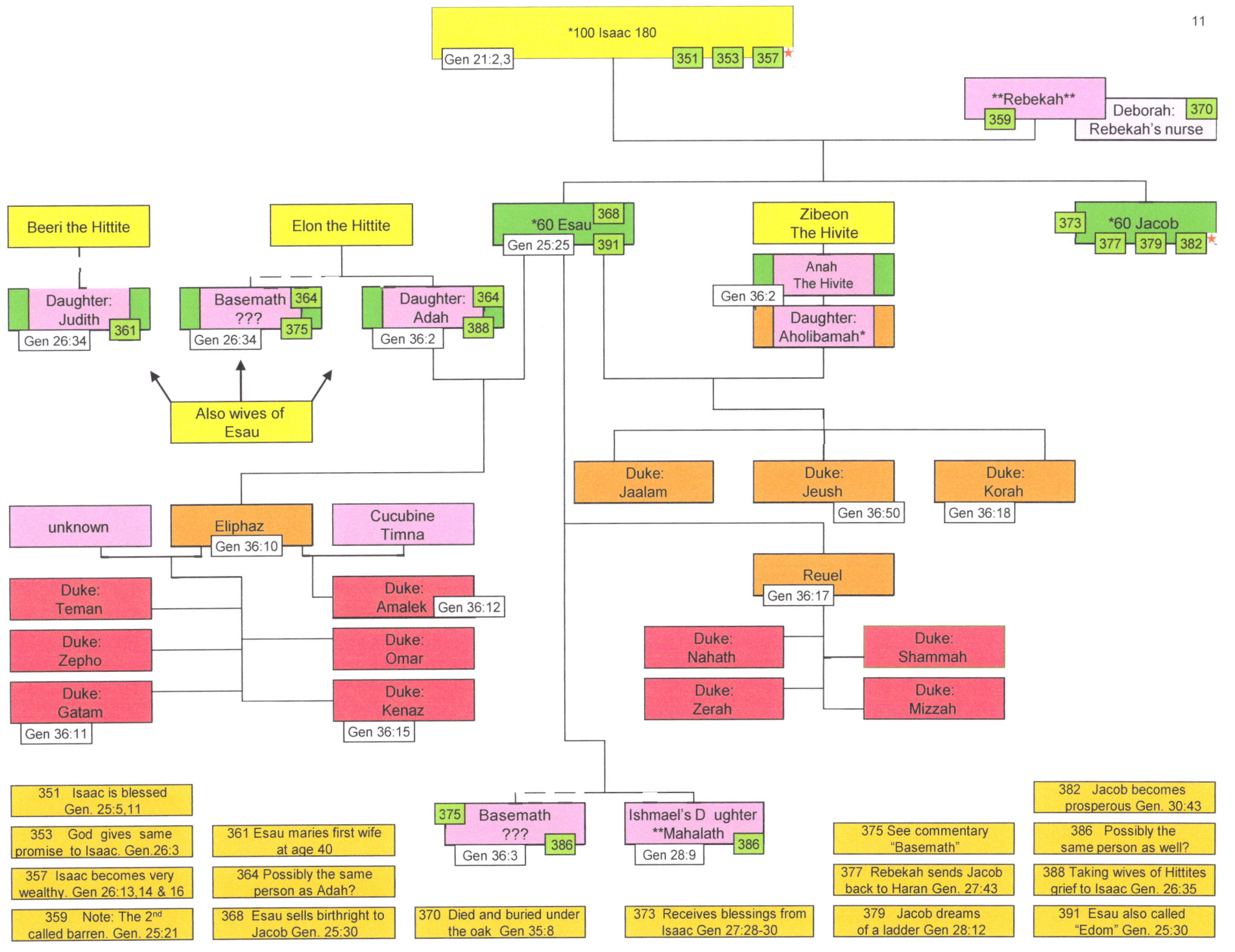

Genesis 36

Basemath

It does seem obvious that God wants to communicate to man through comprehension and understanding of the heart, lacking that of forgetfulness. If God communicates with his people and they, or the next generation forgets, then wherein is the comprehension and understanding that was given to the people from his own heart. The standards would not be kept, the precepts would not be adhered to, and the principles would not be in mind, not to mention reverenced, if all is lost from memory. Walking with God develops an understanding of him. Experience causes a person to know God better. It also causes God to know the person and their heart, allowing God to both reward and judge someone according to their actions as a result of their level of faith. Walking faithfully with God and having experiences with him paints a picture over time, a picture that is painted by God himself. That picture is what we want to see.

Following the Biblical genealogy, and reading chapter 36 of Genesis certainly causes you to desire a better understanding or it might cause you to write it off as a simple contradiction in the bible. I am sure that I speak for God when I say, He does not want you to take the latter route.

According to the account in Genesis, Esau marries three Canaanite women. He goes to his uncle, his grandfather's brother Ishmael, realizing that his father does not approve of him marrying the women of Canaan. So he proposes, for that reason, to marry Mahalath, a non-Canaanite woman, his uncle's daughter (Gen. 28:8-9 and Gen. 26:34).

When reading the scriptures concerning this matter, again there is a desire for clarity. Understand, to be personally convinced of what the scripture is saying you will have to study for yourself and study carefully. While doing so, keep your mind open for an overall understanding.

I would like to show one point of view. Then, in addition, I would like to show some commentary found concerning this.
- In Genesis 26:34, Basemath the daughter of Elon the Hittite, I suggest is Adah, which is his 2nd wife, Judith is the 1st. Esau is now 40 years old.
- In Genesis 36:2, it is stated also, that Adah is the daughter of Elon the Hittite.
- In Genesis 36:2, as well, having been married to Judith already, he marries Adah which the two are a grief to his parents.
- In Genesis 28:9, understanding his parents are disturbed, he marries a woman of Israel, Mahalath the daughter of his grandfather's brother, making her his fourth wife.
- In Genesis 36, and not 26, I suggest that every place that it says Basemath, it is referring to Mahalath. That is confirmed by being the sister of Nebajoth (Gen. 28:9 & Gen. 36:3).
- In Genesis 36:2, it's possible that Aholibamah could be the 4th wife, although this verse suggests a sequence that is befitting to the story.

The text mentions Adah, although it is understood that Judith is his 1st wife at age 40. Then it mentions Aholibamah, which I suggest, is the 3rd wife, again leaving out Judith altogether. Finally, it mentions Basemath the sister of Nebajoth, which most have no problem believing this is Mahalath, the 4th wife with whom an attempt is made, by Esau, to please his parents. Notice in this proposal, there is no person by the birth name of Basemath. It is possible, with the helpful understandings of other commenters, that "Basemath" which is said to mean "fragrance" was a personal term of endearment and a non-birth name used by Esau for two different women. The reason that this is important to understand, is because some have asserted that this, "Basemath or not" question, to be a simple mistake in the Bible. I think not.

Author: Timothy D. McCullough

'...Mahalath, nicknaming her "the Fragrant" to spite Adah. Thus, Esau's various marriages can be plausibly reconstructed as follows:
First wife: Judith, daughter of Beeri the Hittite
Second wife: Adah, "the Fragrant" (Bashemath), daughter of Elon the Hittite; deceased or divorced
Third wife: Mahalath, "the Fragrant" (Bashemath), daughter of Ishmael and sister of Nebajoth
Fourth wife: Aholibamah, granddaughter of Zibeon the Hivite '.

Author: Stephen Caesar

The Land of Seir

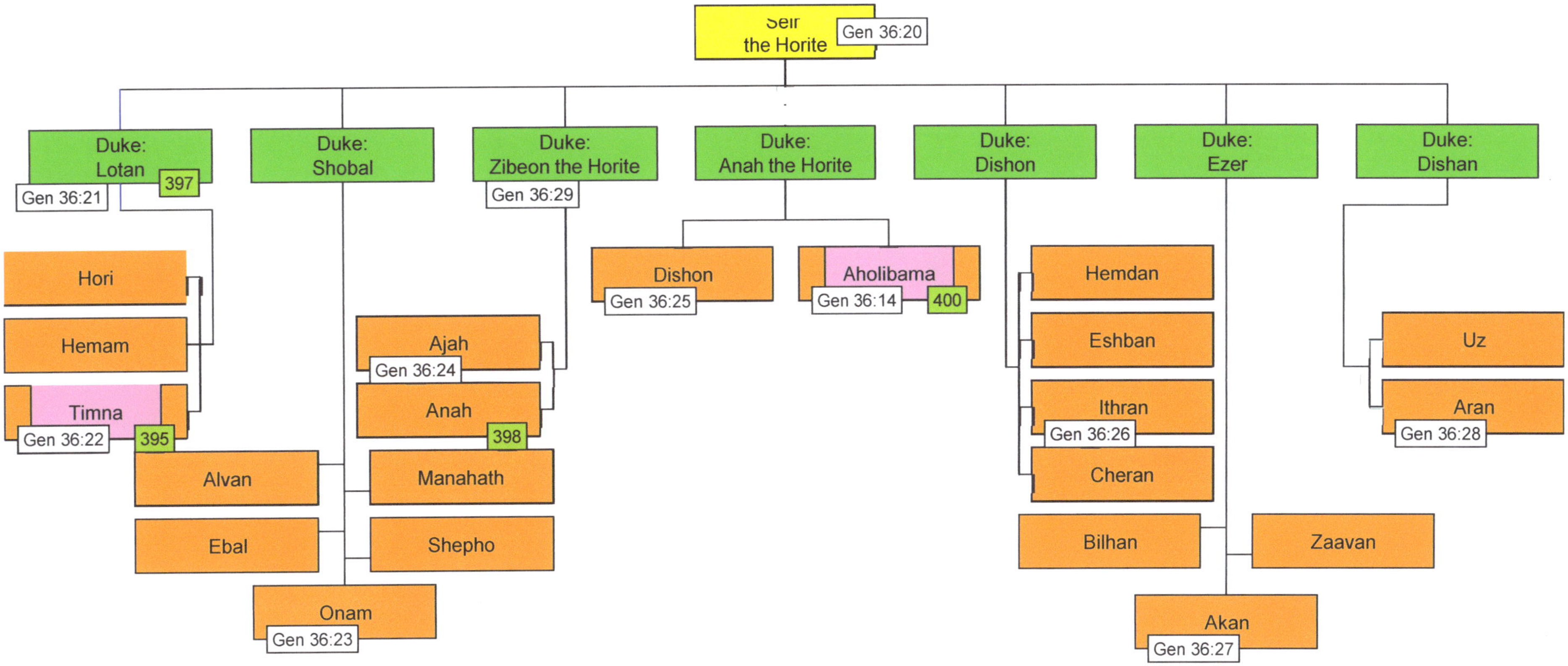

- **Seir the Horite** (Gen 36:20)
  - **Duke: Lotan** (Gen 36:21) [397]
    - Hori
    - Hemam
    - Timna (Gen 36:22) [395]
  - **Duke: Shobal**
    - Alvan
    - Manahath
    - Ebal
    - Shepho
    - Onam (Gen 36:23)
  - **Duke: Zibeon the Horite** (Gen 36:29)
    - Ajah (Gen 36:24)
    - Anah [398]
  - **Duke: Anah the Horite**
    - Dishon (Gen 36:25)
    - Aholibama (Gen 36:14) [400]
  - **Duke: Dishon**
    - Hemdan
    - Eshban
    - Ithran (Gen 36:26)
    - Cheran
  - **Duke: Ezer**
    - Bilhan
    - Zaavan
    - Akan (Gen 36:27)
  - **Duke: Dishan**
    - Uz
    - Aran (Gen 36:28)

---

395 Becomes cucubine to Eliphaz

397 Sir Duke Lotan and his brothers are Seirites because of their father. They are also Horites because of him and his father, just as all of them could be called after their great grand father.

398 This is the Anah that found the mule/hot springs

399 This is the Anah that found the mule

400 Became wife to Esau

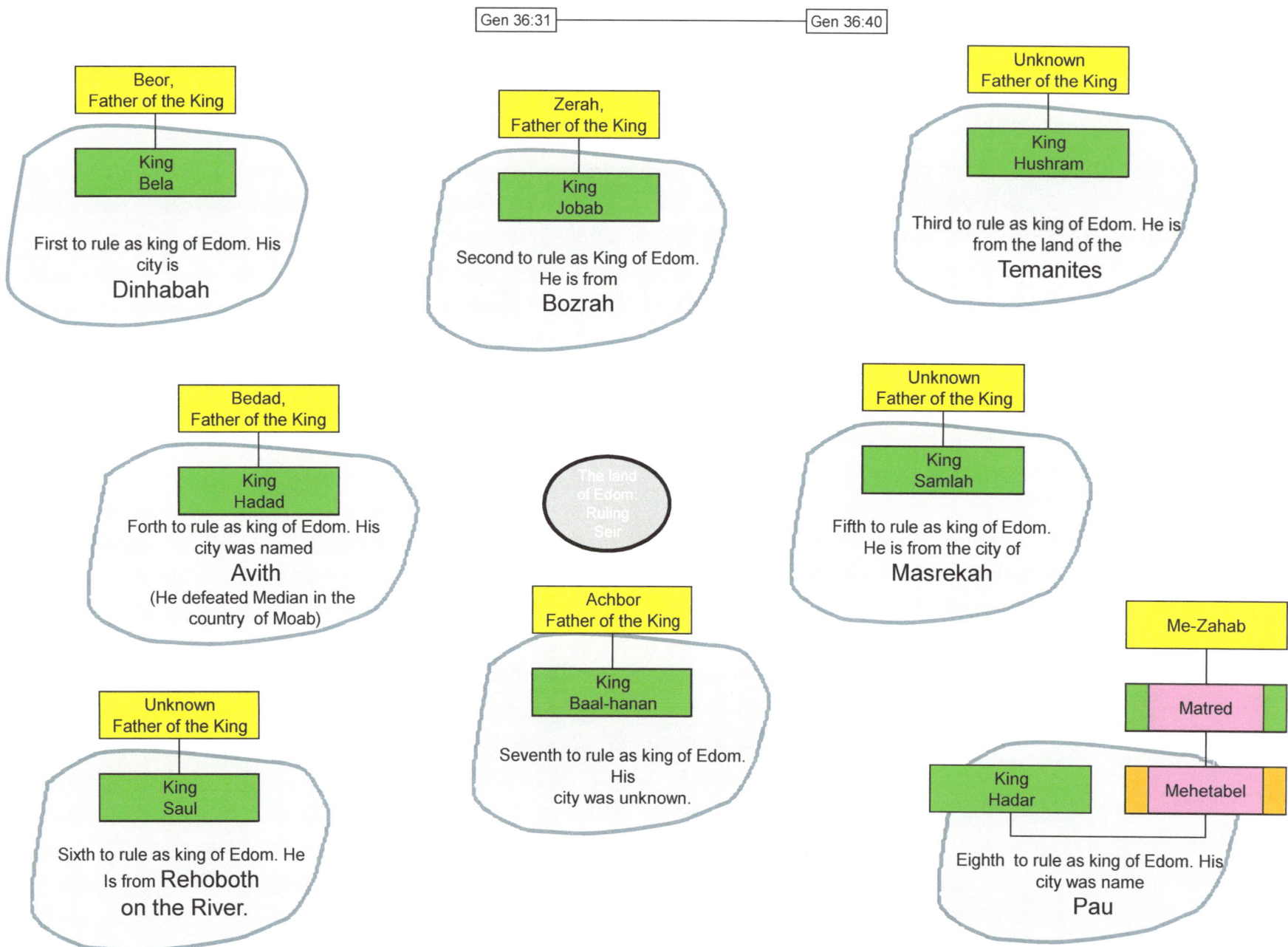

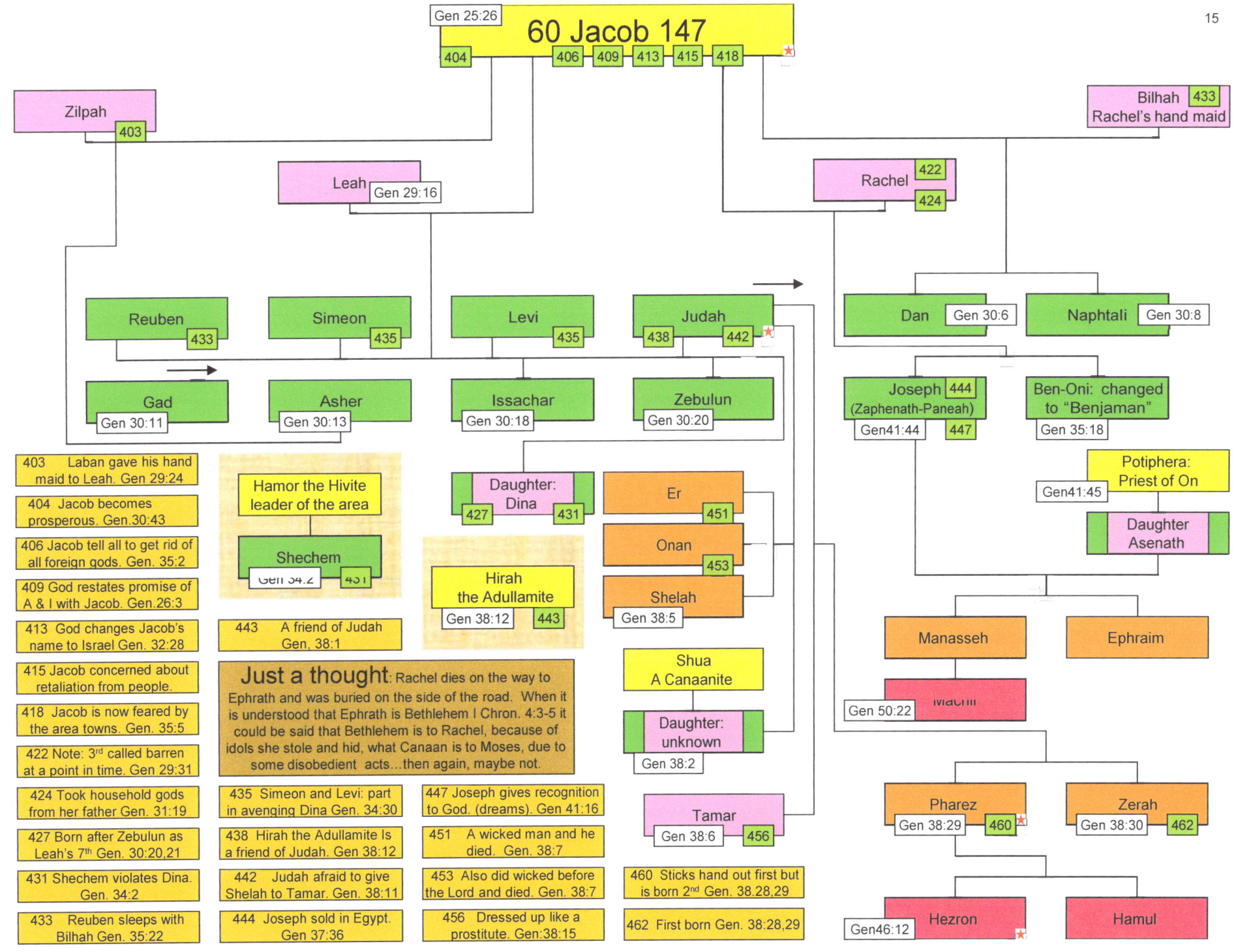

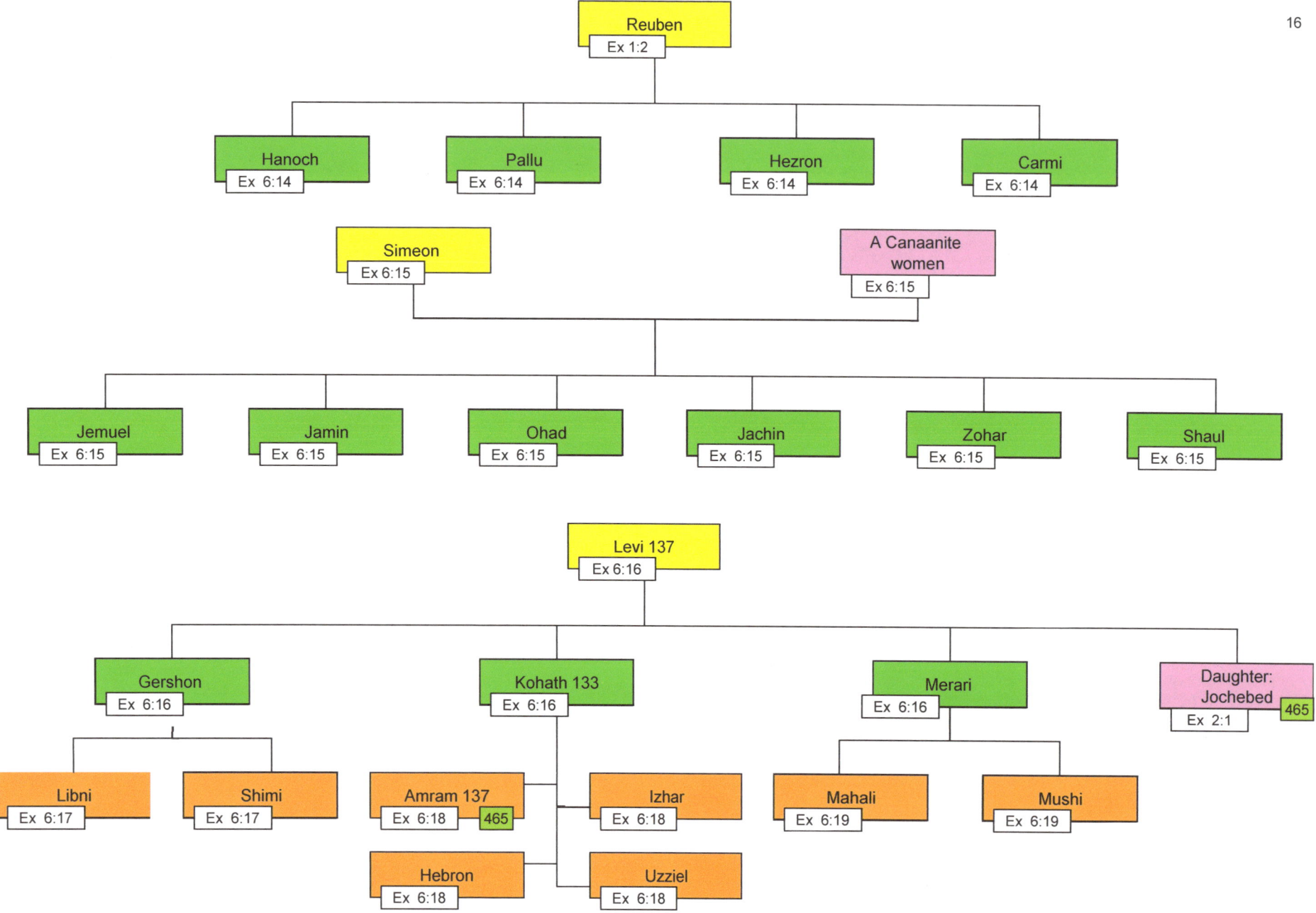

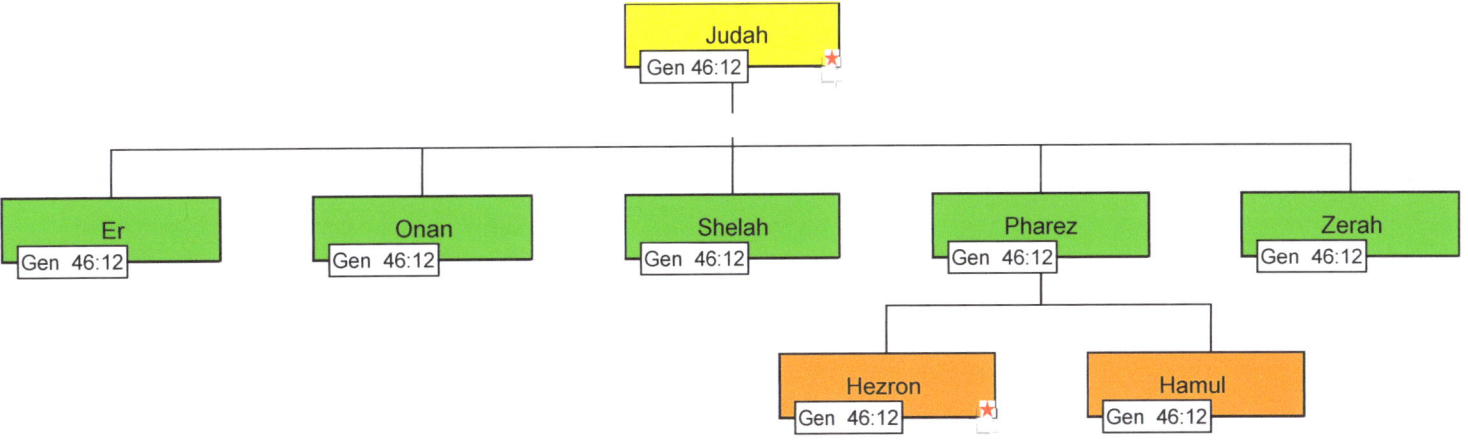
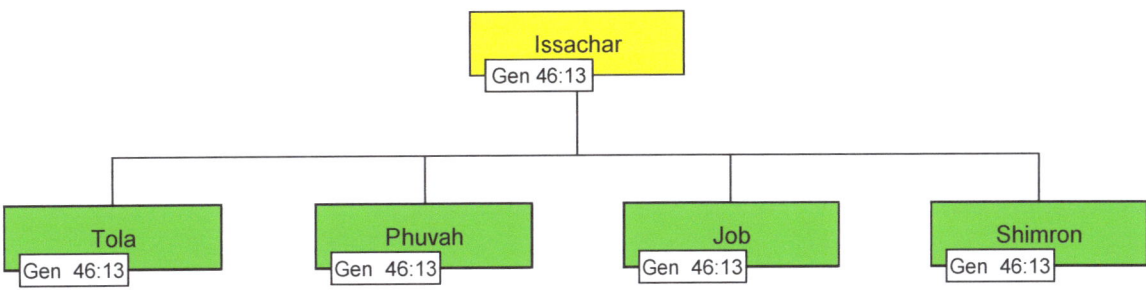
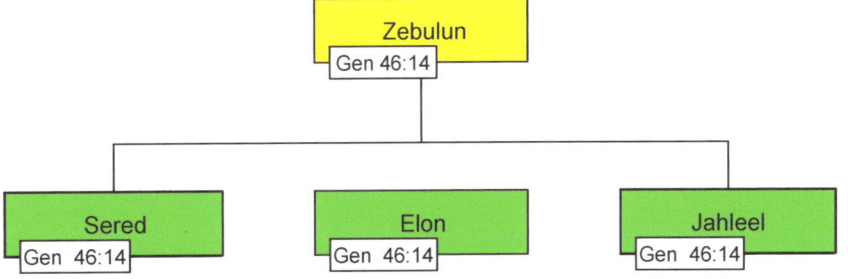

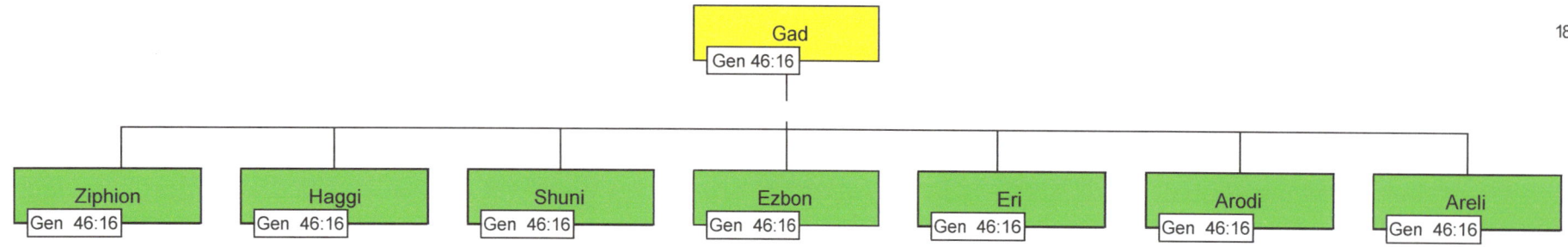
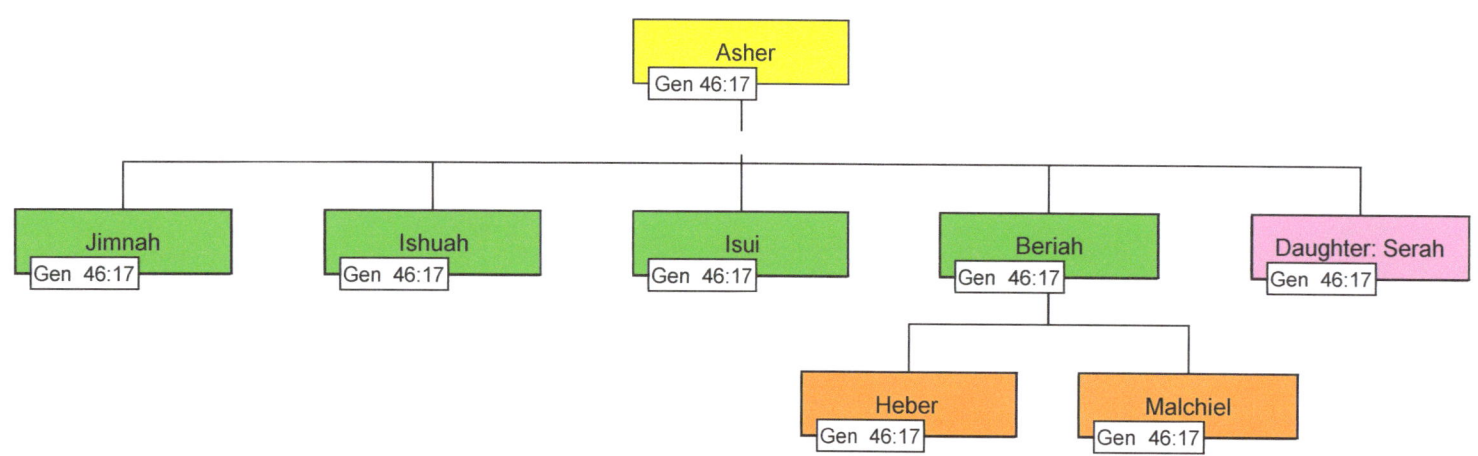
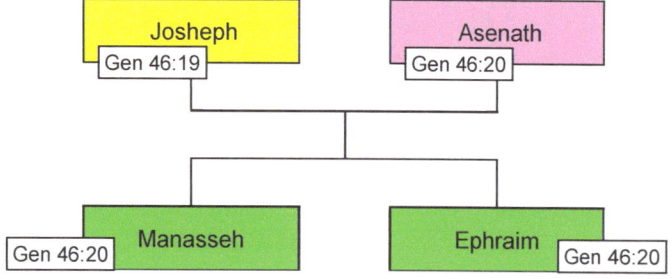

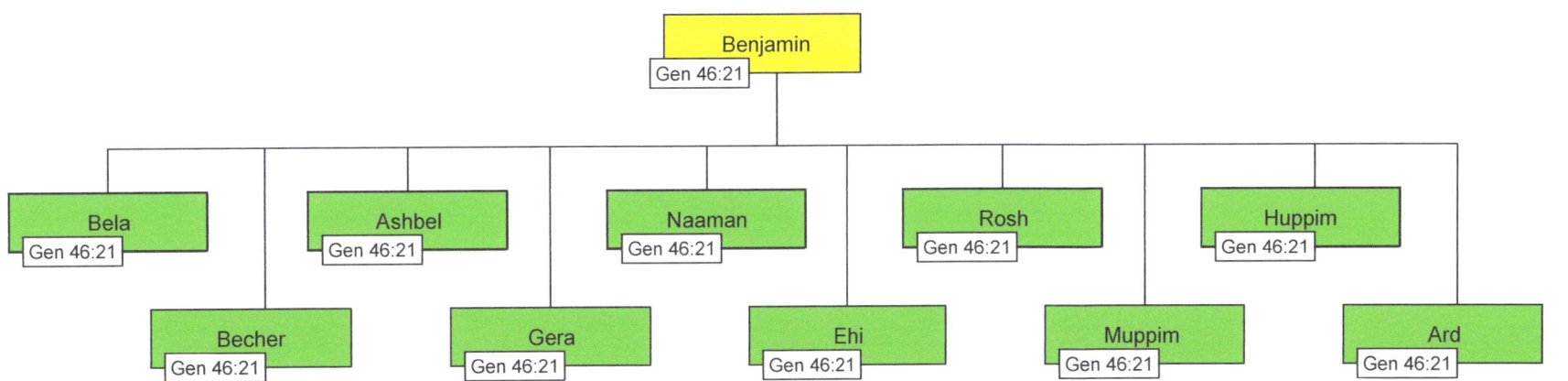
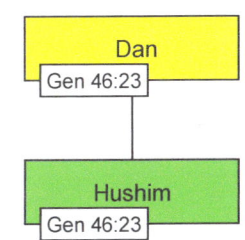
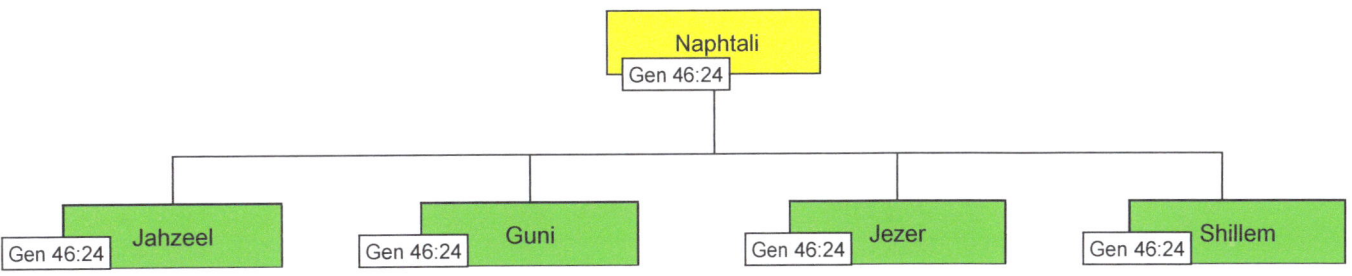

New King over Egypt — 469

Exodus 1 (469)

8 Now there arose up a new king over Egypt, which knew not Joseph. 9 And he said unto his people, Behold, the people of the children of Israel are more and mightier than we: 10 Come on, let us deal wisely with them; lest they multiply, and it come to pass, that, when there falleth out any war, they join also unto our enemies, and fight against us, and so get them up out of the land. 11 Therefore they did set over them taskmasters to afflict them with their burdens. And they built for Pharaoh treasure cities, Pithom and Raamses. 12 But the more they afflicted them, the more they multiplied and grew. And they were grieved because of the children of Israel. KJV

Shiphrah — 471

Puah — 471

471 Ex. 1:15 And the kings of Egypt spake to the Hebrew midwives of which the name of the one was Shiphra, and the name of the other Puah: 16 And said, When ye do the office of a midwife to the Hebrew women, and see them upon the stool; if it be a son, then ye shall kill him: but if it be a daughter, then she shall live. 17 But the midwives feared God, and did not as the king of Egypt commanded them, but saved the men children alive. KJV

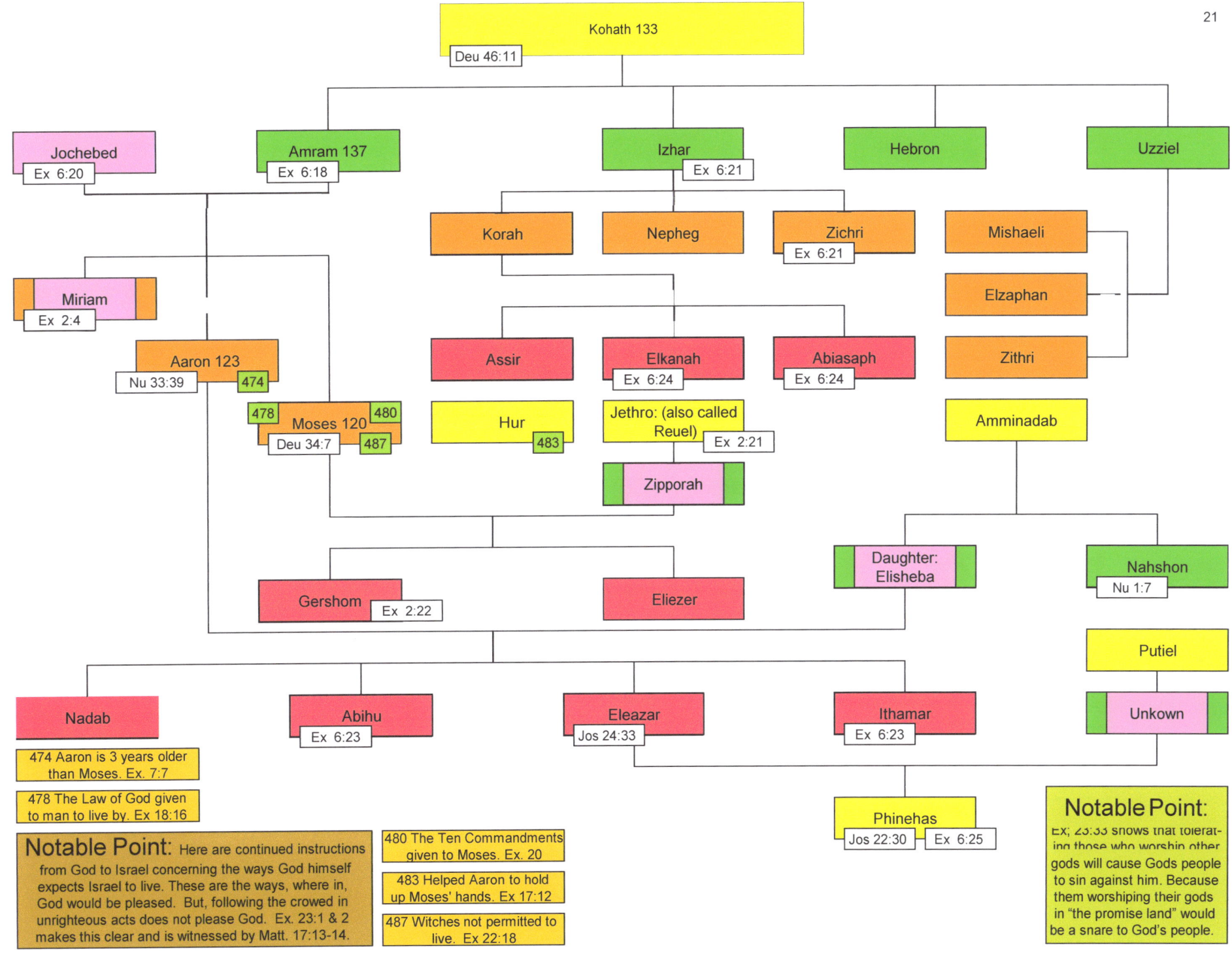

GOD GIVEN TALENT

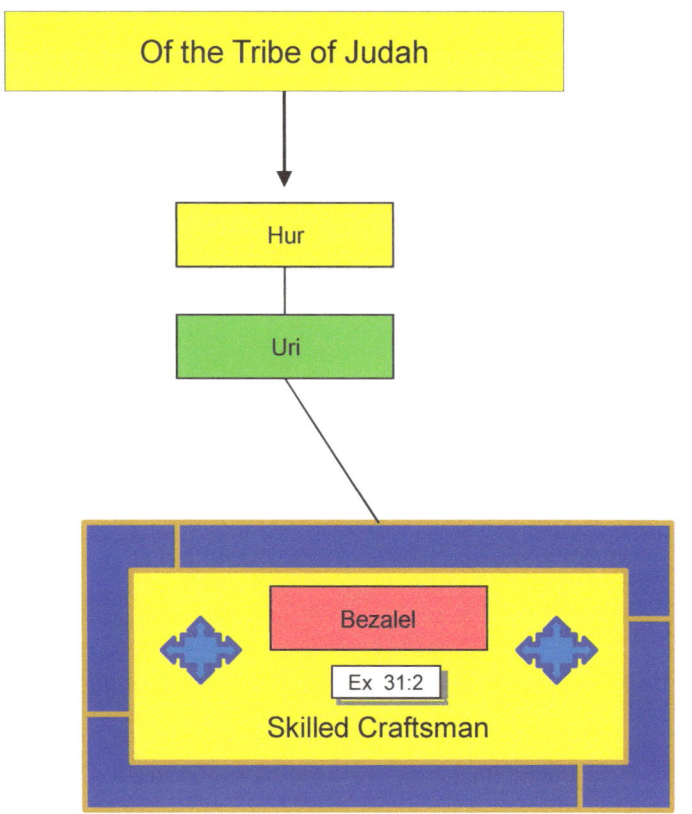

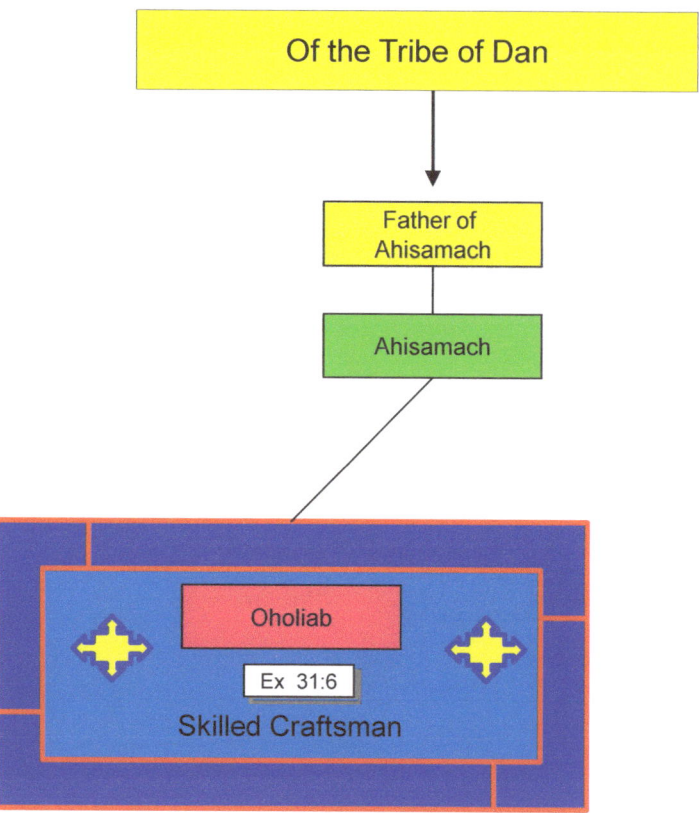

Ex 31
¹ Then the LORD said to Moses, ² "See, I have chosen Bezalel son of Uri, the son of Hur, of the tribe of Judah, ³ and I have filled him with the Spirit of God, with skill, ability and knowledge in all kinds of crafts ⁴ to make artistic designs for work in gold, silver and bronze, ⁵ to cut and set stones, to work in wood, and to engage in all kinds of craftsmanship. ⁶ Moreover, I have appointed Oholiab son of Ahisamach, of the tribe of Dan, to help him.

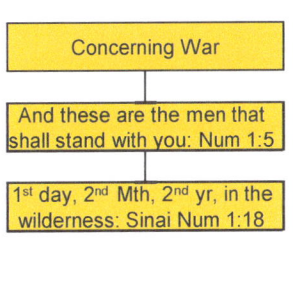

Concerning War

And these are the men that shall stand with you: Num 1:5

1st day, 2nd Mth, 2nd yr, in the wilderness: Sinai Num 1:18

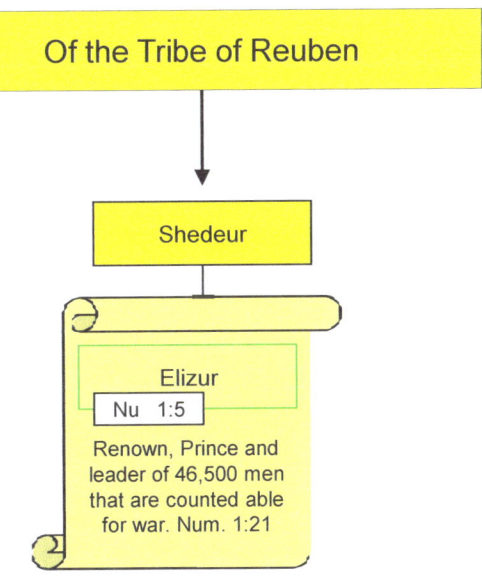

Of the Tribe of Reuben

Shedeur

Elizur — Nu 1:5

Renown, Prince and leader of 46,500 men that are counted able for war. Num. 1:21

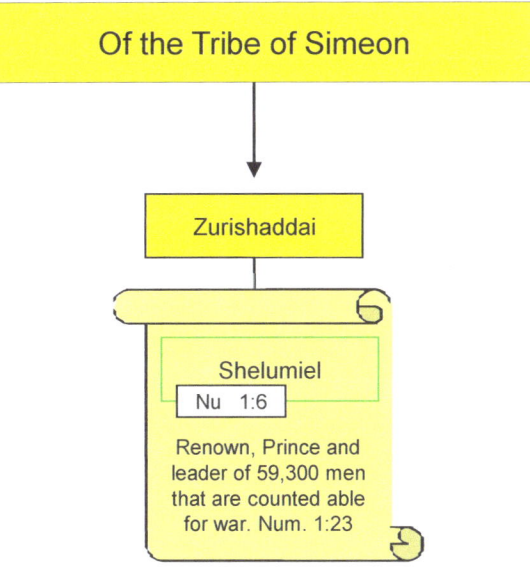

Of the Tribe of Simeon

Zurishaddai

Shelumiel — Nu 1:6

Renown, Prince and leader of 59,300 men that are counted able for war. Num. 1:23

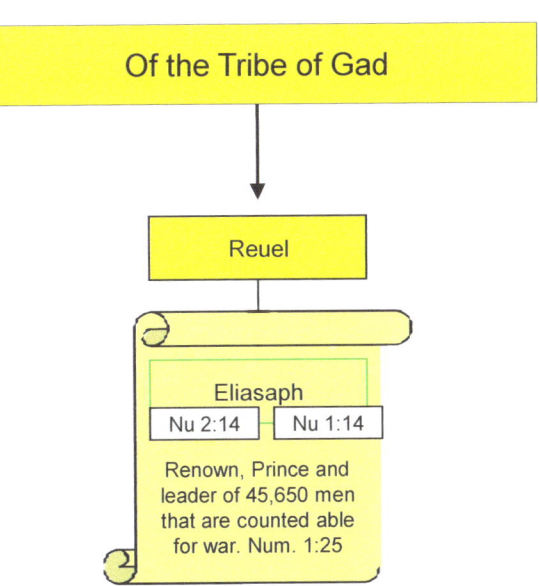

Of the Tribe of Gad

Reuel

Eliasaph — Nu 2:14 | Nu 1:14

Renown, Prince and leader of 45,650 men that are counted able for war. Num. 1:25

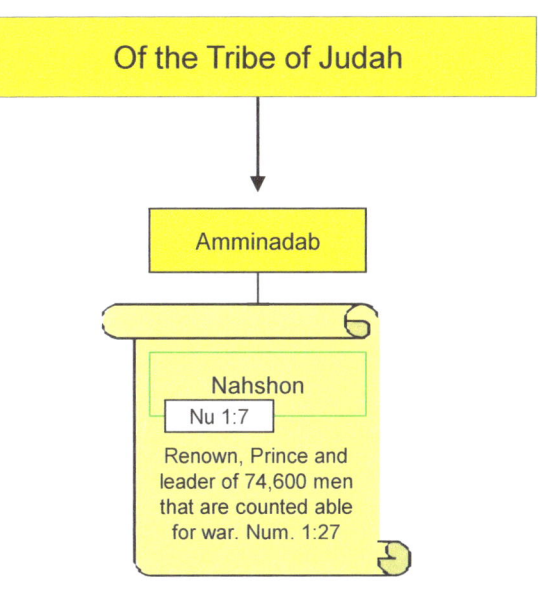

Of the Tribe of Judah

Amminadab

Nahshon — Nu 1:7

Renown, Prince and leader of 74,600 men that are counted able for war. Num. 1:27

Concerning War

And these are the men that shall stand with you: Num 1:5

1st day, 2nd Mth, 2nd yr, in the Wilderness: Sinai Num 1:18

Of the Tribe of Issachar

Zuar

Nethaneel — Nu 1:8

Renown, Prince and leader of 54,400 men that are counted able for war. Num. 1:29

Of the Tribe of Zebulun

Helon

Eliab — Nu 1:9

Renown, Prince and leader of 57,400 men that are counted able for war. Num. 1:31

Of the Sons of Joseph

Ephraim

Ammihud

Elishama — Nu 1:10

Renown, Prince and leader of 40,500 men that are counted able for war. Num. 1:33

Mannasseh

Pedahzur

Gamaliel — Nu 1:10

Renown, Prince and leader of 32,200 men that are counted able for war. Num. 1:35

Of the Tribe of Benjamin

Gideoni

Abidan — Nu 1:11

Renown, Prince and leader of 35,400 men that are counted able for war. Num. 1:37

Of the Tribe of Dan	Of the Tribe of Asher	Of the Tribe of Naphtali
Ammishaddai	Ocran	Enan
Ahiezer — Nu 1:12	Pegiel — Nu 1:13	Ahira — Nu 1:15
Renown, Prince and leader of 62,700 men that are counted able for war. Num. 1:39	Renown, Prince and leader of 41,500 men that are counted able for war. Num. 1:41	Renown, Prince and leader of 53,400 men that are counted able for war. Num. 1:43

The Tribe of Levi

Are not counted for war
Numbers 1: 47-53

Numbers Chapter 3…
6. Bring the tribe of Levi near, and present them before Aaron the priest, that they may minister unto him.
7. And they shall keep his charge, and the charge of the whole congregation before the tabernacle of the congregation, to do the service of the tabernacle.

Males of Levi numbered, mth old & up; 22,000 Num. 3: 39

God has shown that he is conscience of numbers. It is either that or numbers just have a way of indicating when God has been operating.

Because of the instruction that he has given to Moses and due to the numbers that are shown in Genesis, we have a time line of Adam's life. And it even goes on after his life.

The book of Numbers deals a lot with counting and accountability. The first chapter starts with God giving Moses a charge to get a sum, the total number of men twenty years and older who are able for war.

The House Of Levi

Levi 137

Gershon
- **Libni** → Libnites Num. 3:21
- **Shimei** → Shimites Num. 3:21

Gershonites Num. 3:21

Eliasaph, son of Lael, Chief of the house of the father of the Gershonites: number of males a mth old and up: 7,500. Num. 3:24

Kohath 133
- **Amram** → Amramites Num. 3:27
- **Izehar** → Izeharites Num. 3:27
- **Hebron** → Hebronites 3:27
- **Uzziel** → Uzzielites Num. 3:27

Kohathites Num. 3:27

Elizaphan, son of Uzziel, Chief of the house of the father of the Kohathites; number of males a mth old and up 8,600. Num. 3:28,30

Merari
- **Mahli** → Mahlites Num. 3:33
- **Mushi** → Mushites Num. 3:33

Merari Family Num. 3:33

Zuriel, son of Abihail, Chief of the house of the father of the families of Merari: number of males a mth old and up, 6,200 Num. 3:34

Levites Num. 3:20

Eleazar, son of Aaron, Chief over the chief of the Levites; number of males a mth old and up: 22,000. Num. 3:39

Numbers Chapter 11: 11-14 & 16,17

11 And Moses said unto the LORD, Wherefore hast thou afflicted thy servant? and wherefore have I not found favour in thy sight, that thou layest the burden of all this people upon me? 12 Have I conceived all this people? have I begotten them, that thou shouldest say unto me, carry them in thy bosom, as a nursing father beareth the sucking child, unto the land which thou swarest unto their fathers?... KJV

13 Whence should I have flesh to give unto all this people? for they weep unto me, saying, Give us flesh, that we may eat. 14 I am not able to bear all this people alone, because it is too heavy for me.

16 And the LORD said unto Moses, Gather unto me seventy men of the elders of Israel, whom thou knowest to be the elders of the people, and officers over them; and bring them unto the Tabernacle of the congregation, that they may stand there with thee. 17 And I will come down and talk with thee there: and I will take of the spirit which is upon thee, and will put it upon them; and they shall bear the burden of the people with thee, that thou bear it not thyself alone. KJV

Isaiah 1:8

"Come now, let us reason together," says the LORD. "Though your sins are like scarlet, they shall be as white as snow; though they are red as crimson, they shall be like wool. KJV

Just a Note

Although God does not change and will not change who he is, Moses demonstrated that after being obedient to God and his purpose, that it is possible to go to him in authenticity of heart and expressingly release your concerns with an understandable hope of a resolution. Isaiah 1:8 also shows a measurement of God's character and his attitude towards man when he himself said, "Come now, let us reason together."

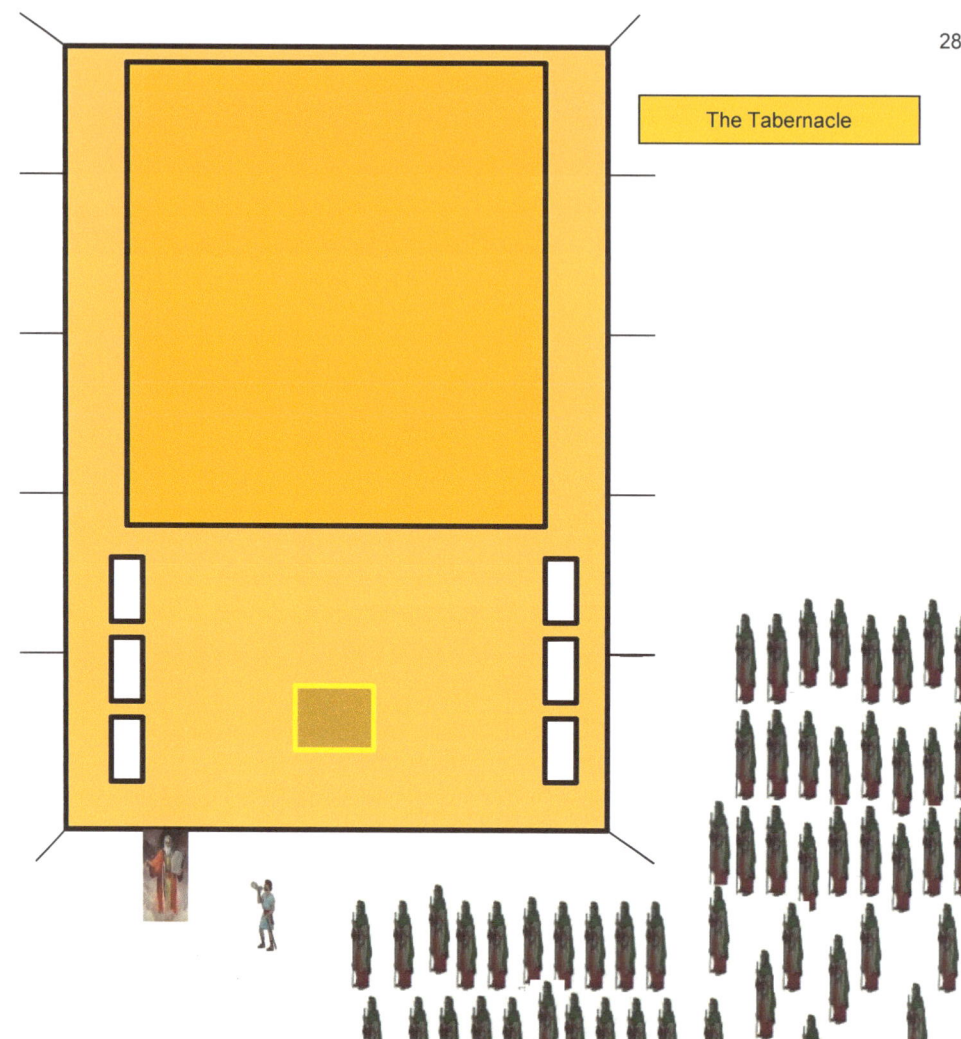

The Tabernacle

Eldad 489

Medad Nu 11:26 489

489 Stayed behind and prophesied Numbers. 11:26

Just a Note: From Numbers 12

Miriam and Aaron complains about Moses having marred an Ethiopian Women in v1. Note v3, Moses being meek. If the Lord wants to respond to a wrong or an enemy then "let God", suggestively, by being meek and humble: fighting when he says fight and holding you peace when he says hold your peace. God gets angry. V9, Miriam becomes leprous. v10 Aaron repents. v11 Moses, whom was spoken against, prays for the one who spoke against him. V13 Miriam restored & v14

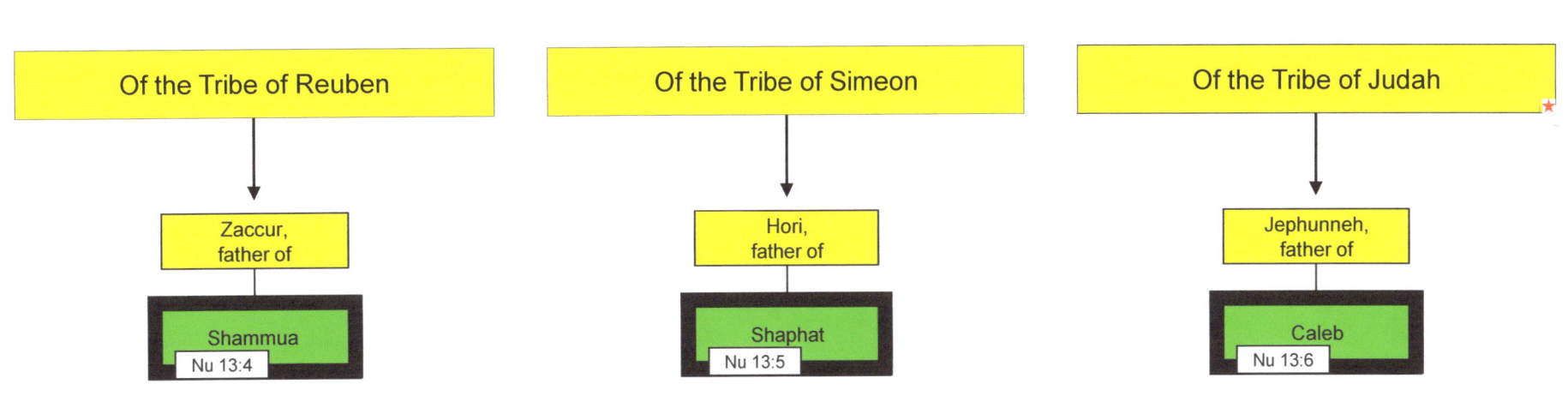
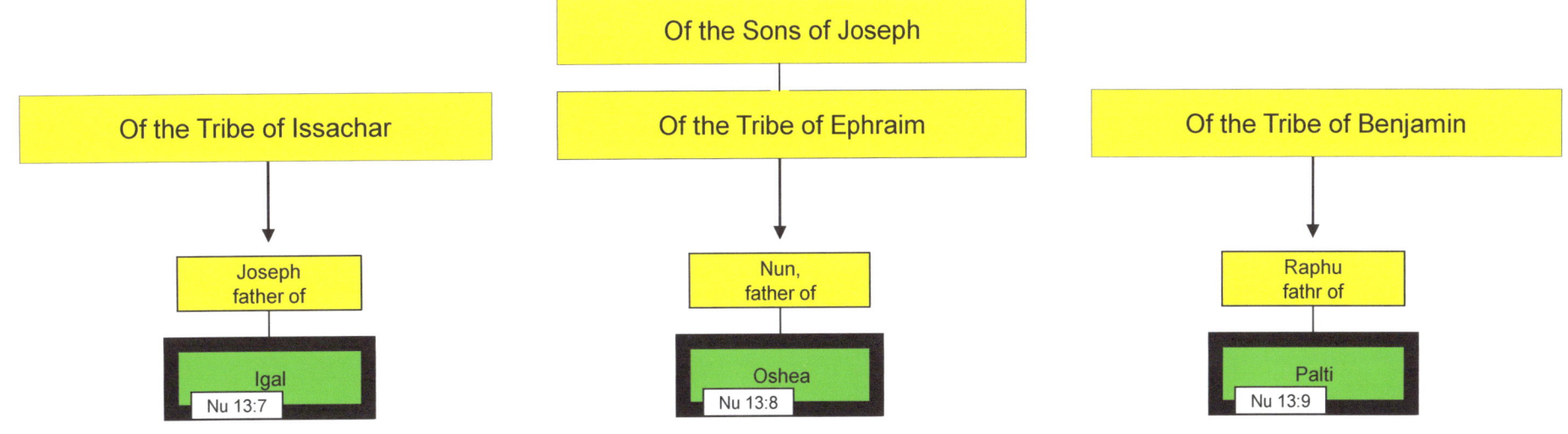

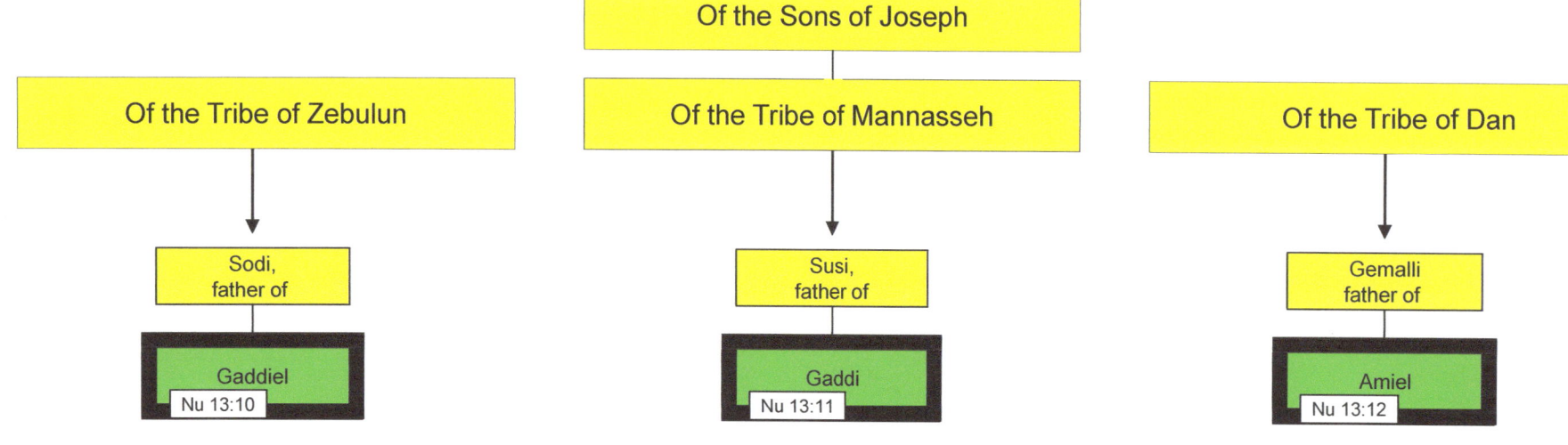
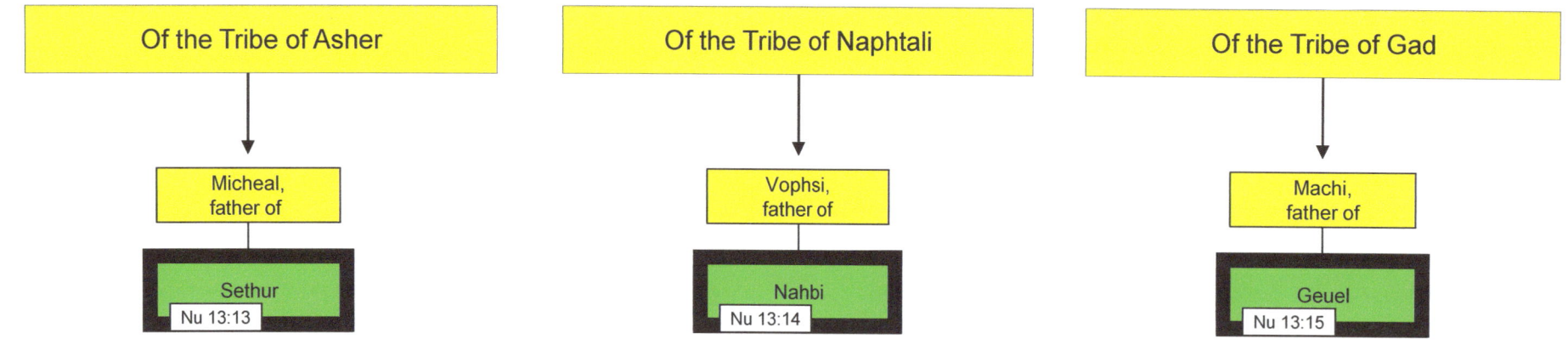

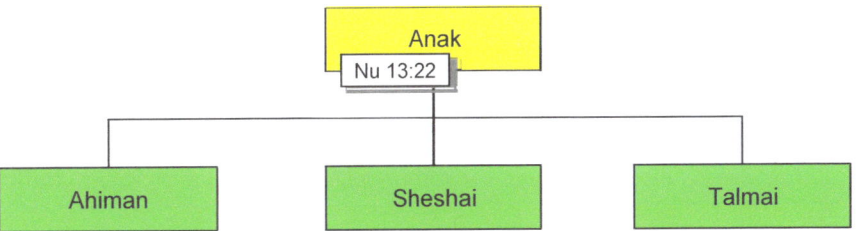

Numbers 13
33 and there have we seen giants -- the sons of Anak are of the giants -- and we were in our sight as grasshoppers, and so we were also in their sight.

Deuteronomy 3
[11] Og, the king of Bashan, was the only Rephaite left. His bed was made out of iron. It was more than 13 feet long and six feet wide. It is still in the Ammonite city of Rabbah.

The faltered opposition against Moses and Aaron

Numbers 16

- Of the Tribe of Reuben → Eliab → Nemuel (Nu 26:9)
- Of the Tribe of Levi
- Peleth

250 Men:
- Korah — 492, 501 (Nu 16:1, Nu 26:10)
- On — 496, 501
- Dathan — 496, 498, 501 (Nu 16:12)
- Abiram — 498, 501 (Nu 16:12)
- 505

Moses and Aaron

Pubic domain

Legend:
- 492 Lead 250 men to confront Moses Nu 16:1-3
- 496 Gave little reverence to Moses & Aaron
- 498 Refused the beckon call of Moses Nu 16:12
- 501 Swallowed up by the ground Nu 16:31-32
- 505 Consumed by fire from the Lord Nu 16:35

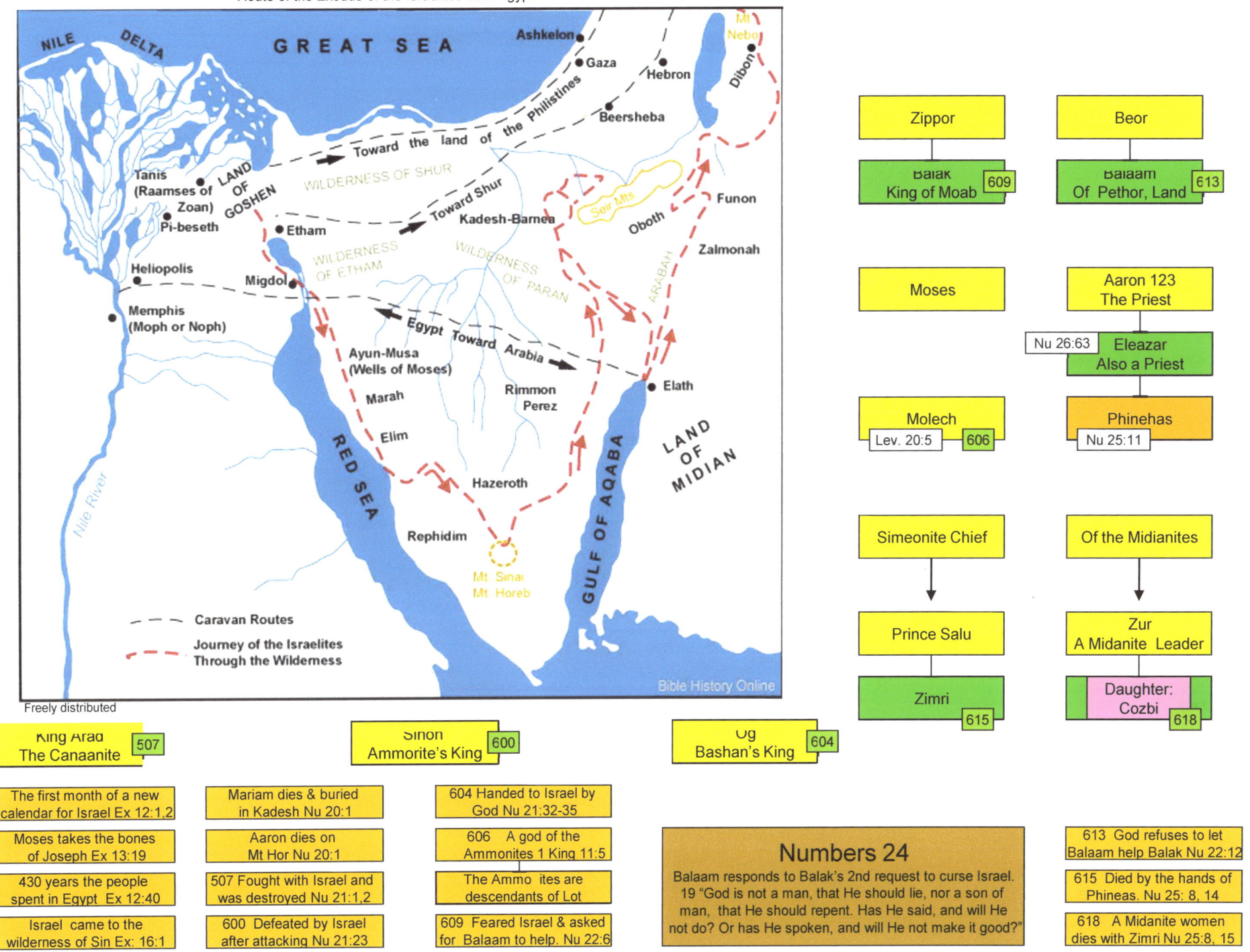

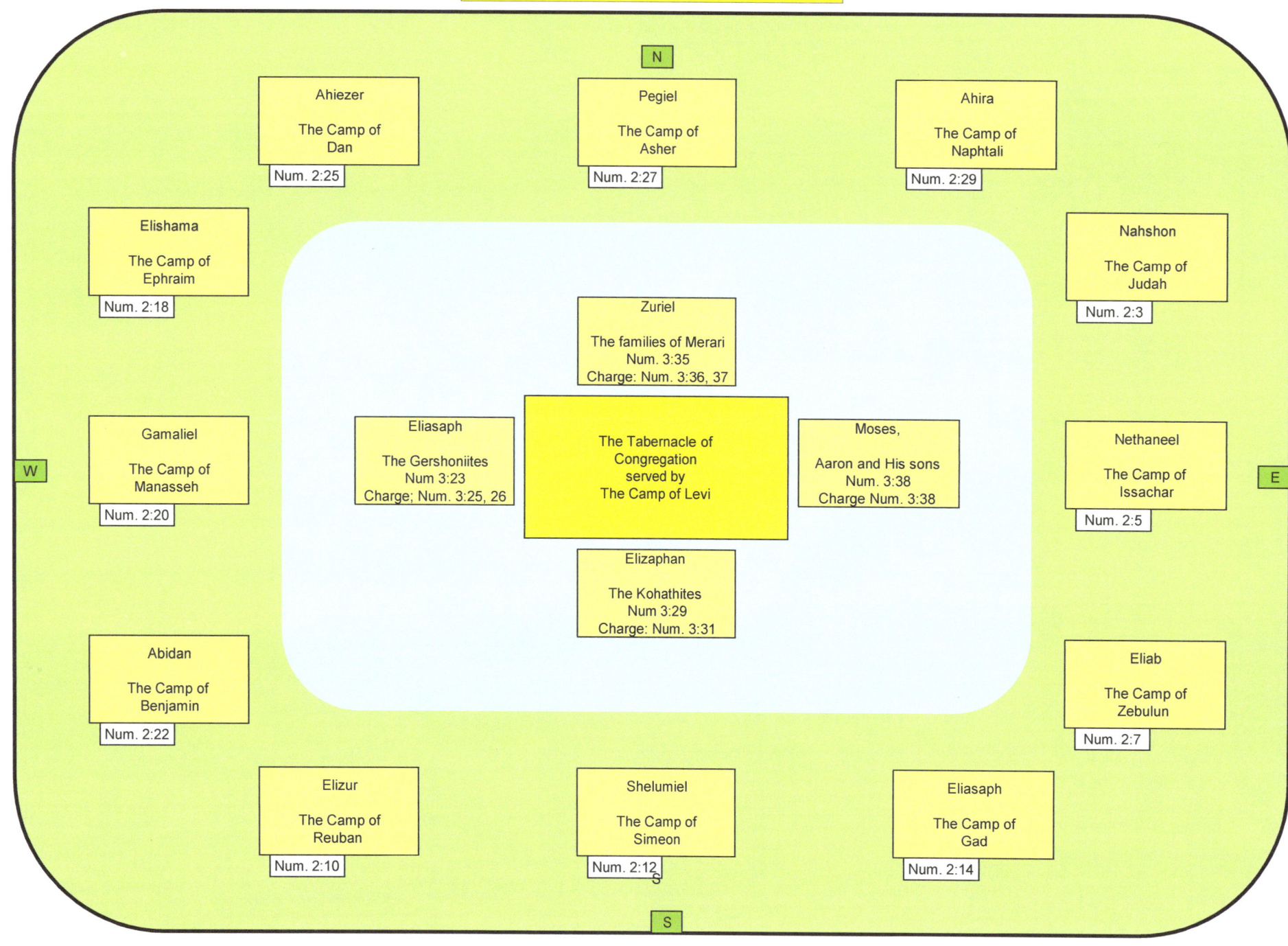

[2] Take ye the sum of all the congregation of the children of Israel, after their families, by the house of their fathers, with the number of their names, every male by their polls;
[3] From twenty years old and upward, all that are able to go forth to war in Israel: thou and Aaron shall number them by their armies.

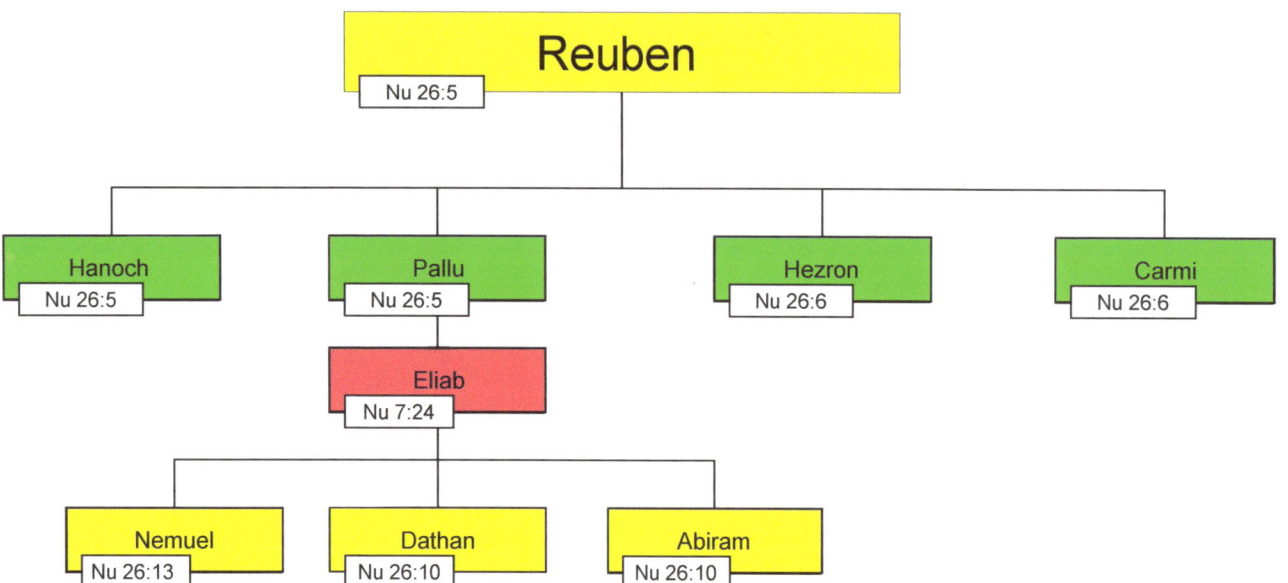

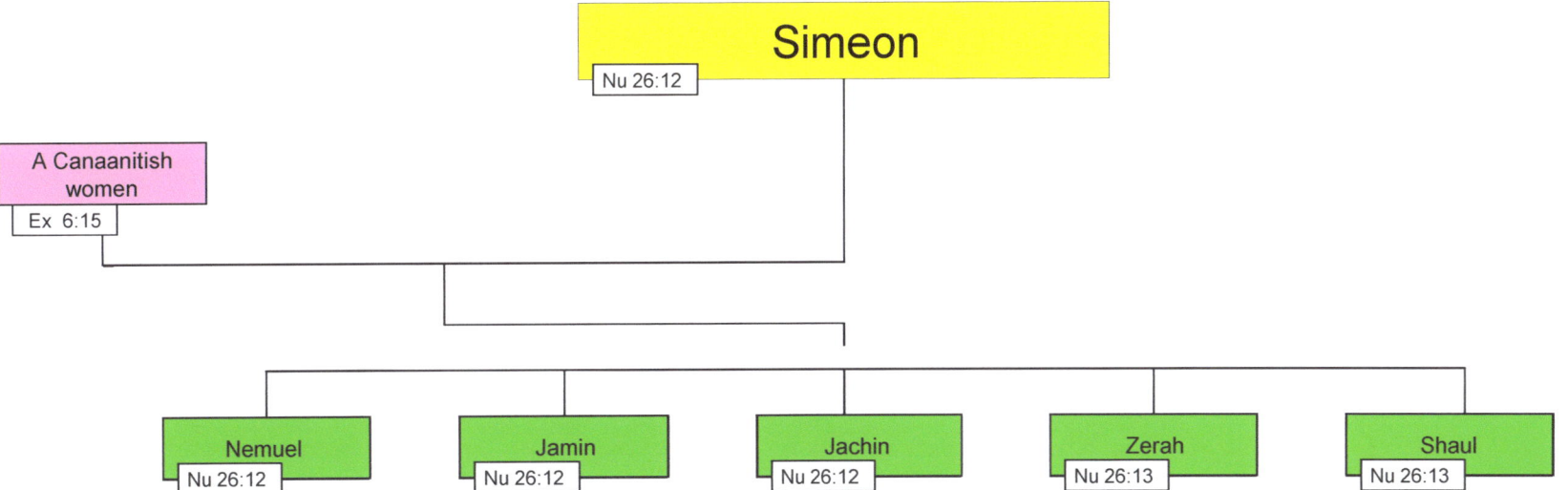

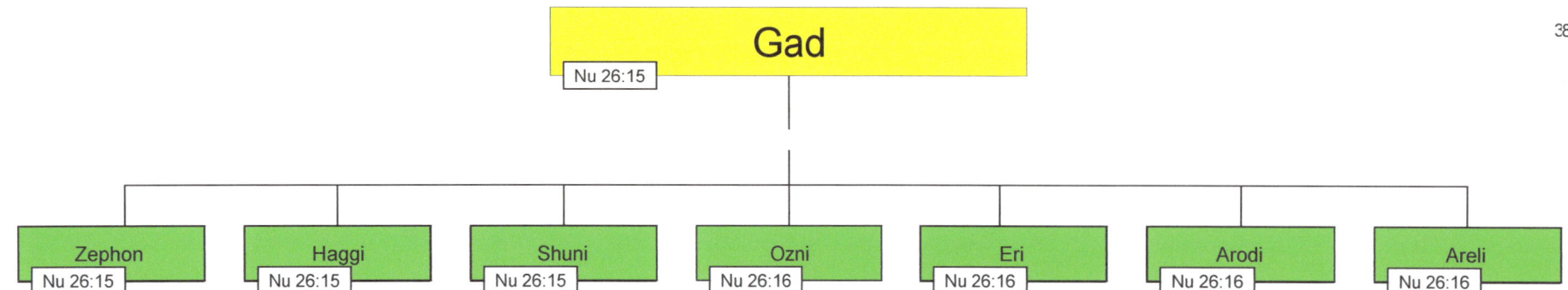

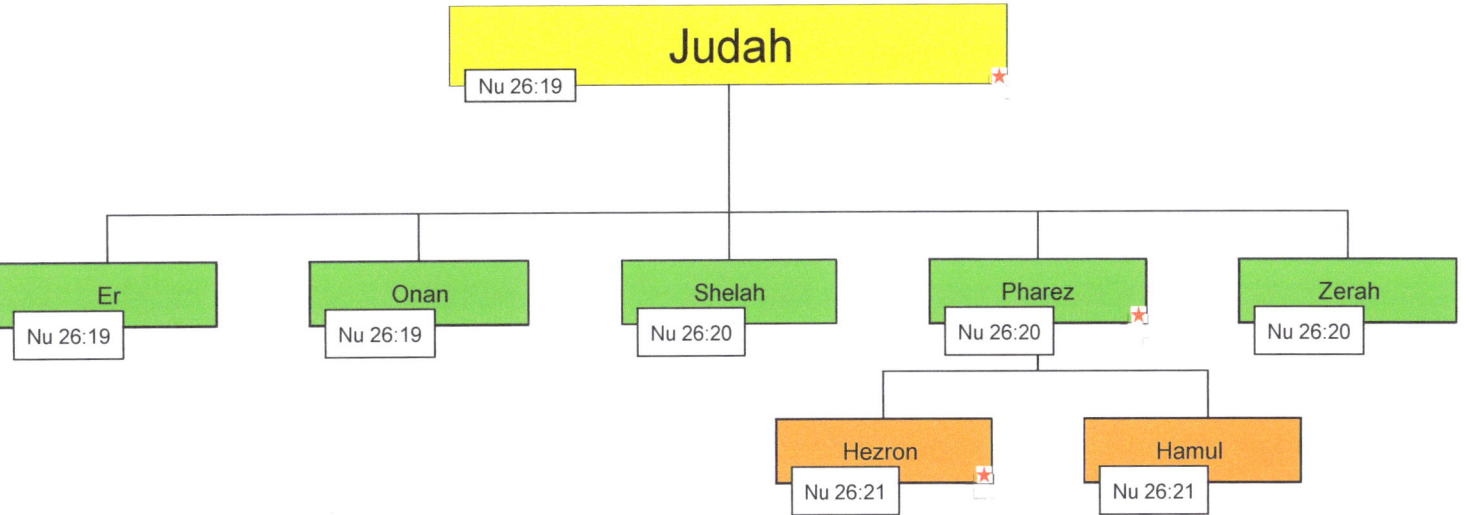

Issachar
Nu 26:23

- **Tola** — Nu 26:23
- **Pua** — Nu 26:23
- **Jashub** — Nu 26:24
- **Shimron** — Nu 26:24

The tribe of Issachar man count: 64,300
Nu 26:25

Zebulun
Gen 46:14

- **Sered** — Nu 26:26
- **Elon** — Nu 26:26
- **Jahleel** — Nu 26:26

The tribe of Zebulun man count: 60,500
Nu 26:27

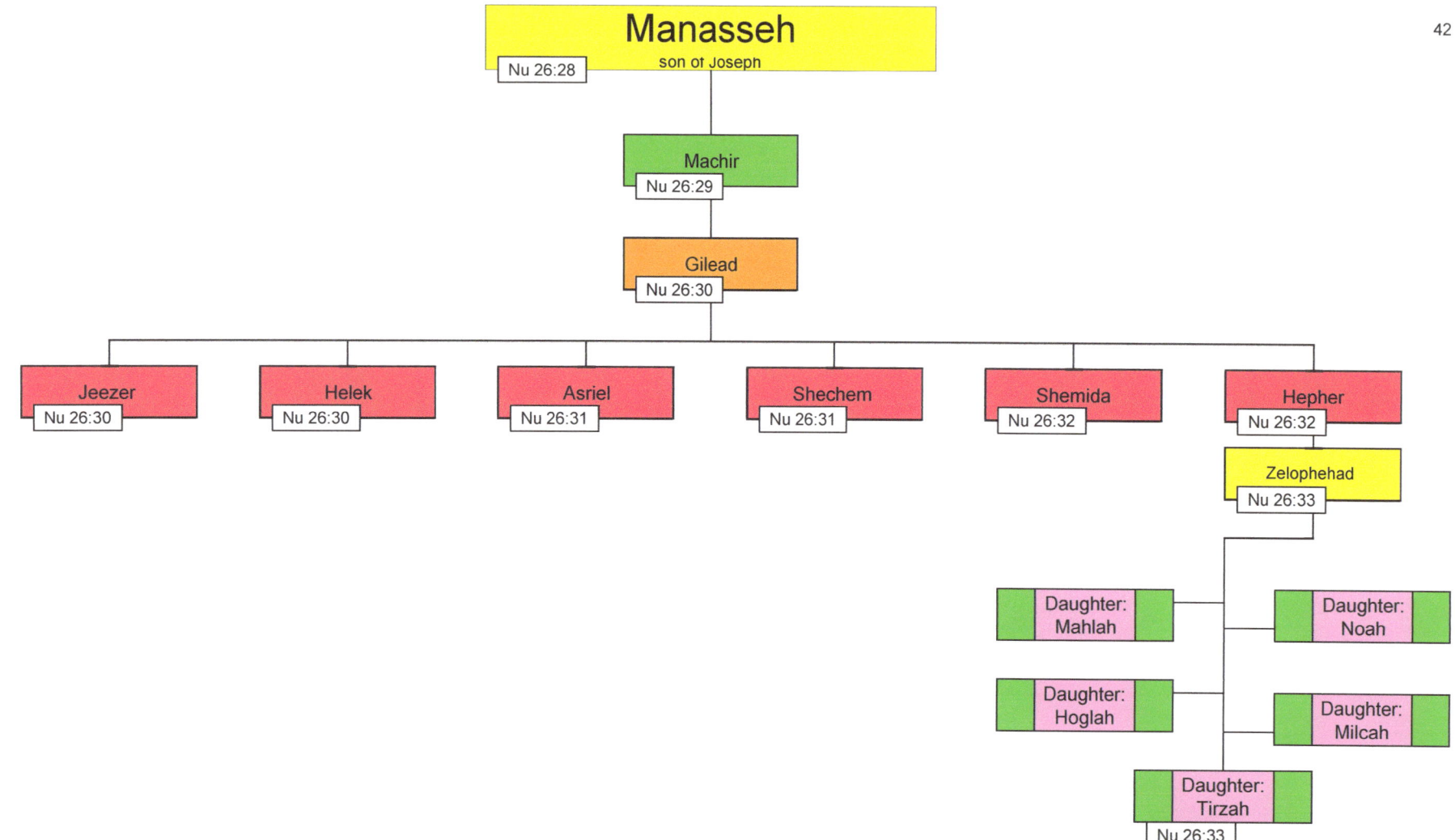

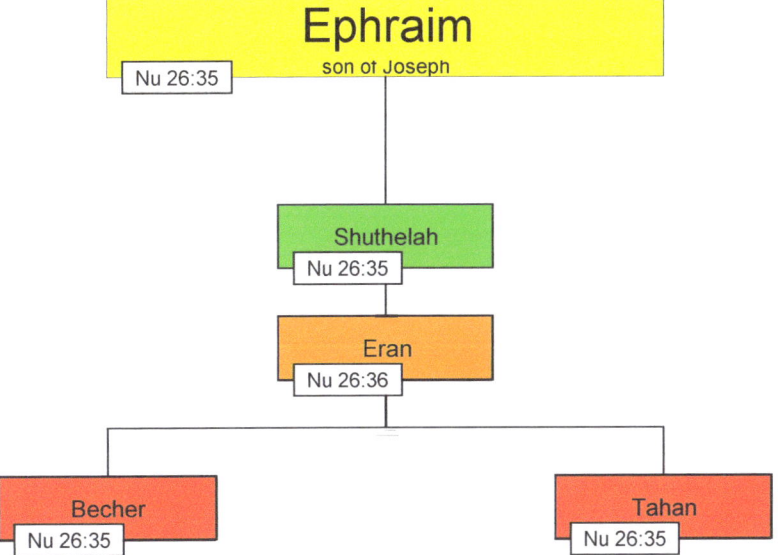

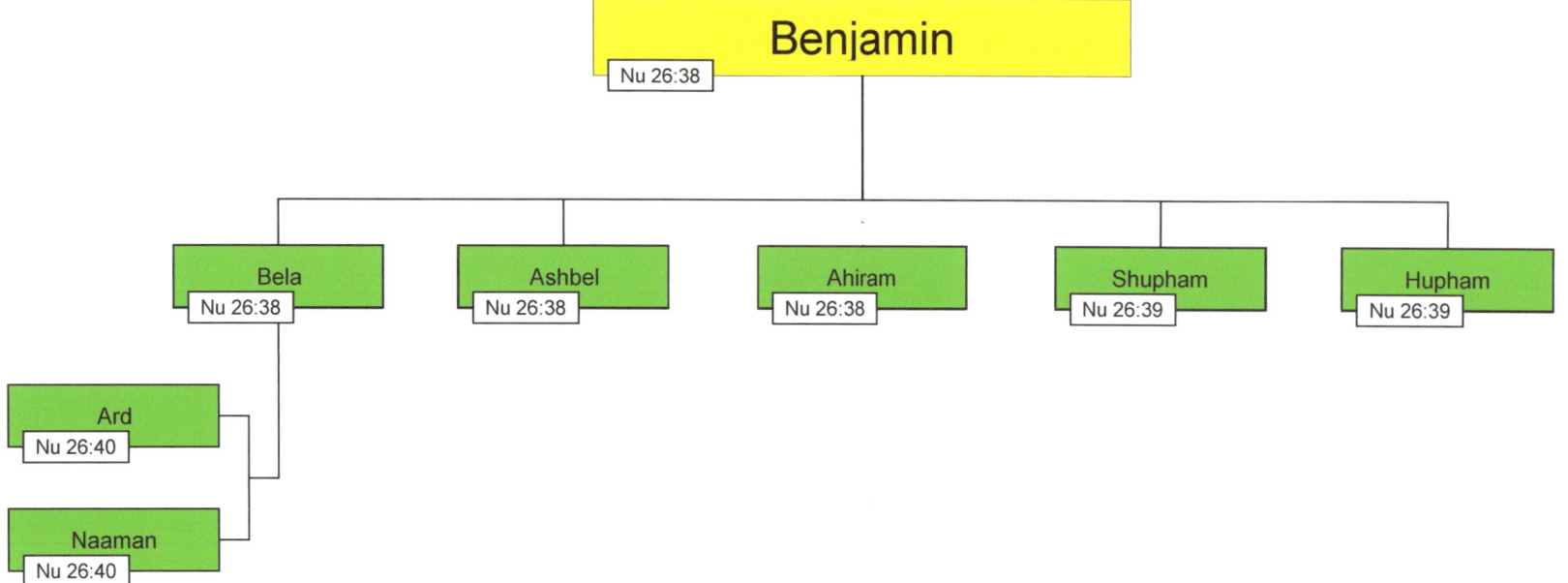

```
Dan
Nu 26:42
  |
Shuham
Nu 26:42
```

The tribe of Dan man count: 64,400
Nu 26:43

Asher
Nu 26:44

- **Jimna** — Nu 26:44
- **Jesui** — Nu 26:44
- **Beriah** — Nu 26:44
  - **Heber** — Nu 26:45
  - **Malchiel** — Nu 26:45
- **Daughter: Serah** — Nu 26:46

The tribe of Asher man count: 53,400
Nu 26:47

```
Naphtali
Nu 26:48
├── Jahzeel (Nu 26:48)
├── Guni (Nu 26:48)
├── Jezer (Nu 26:49)
└── Shillem (Nu 26:49)
```

The tribe of Naphtali man count: 45,400
Nu 26:50

Numbers 25

16 And the LORD spake unto Moses, saying,
17 Vex the Midianites, and smite them:
18 For they vex you with their wiles, wherewith they have beguiled you in the matter of Peor, and in the matter of Cozbi, the daughter of a prince of Midian, their sister, which was slain in the day of the plague for Peor's sake. KJV

Numbers 31

16 Behold, these caused the children of Israel, through the counsel of Balaam, to commit trespass gainst the LORD in the matter of Peor, and there was a plague among the congregation of the LORD. KJV

Taking Note: Numbers 31

v48 And the officers which were over thousands of the host, the captains of thousands, and captains of hundreds, came near unto Moses:
vv49 And they said unto Moses, Thy servants have taken the sum of the men of war which are under our charge, and there lacketh not one man of us. (KJV)

v50 We have therefore brought an oblation for the LORD, what every man hath gotten, of jewels of gold, chains, and bracelets, rings, earrings, and tablets, to make an atonement for our souls before the LORD.
v51 And Moses and Eleazar the priest took the gold of them, even all wrought jewels. (KJV)

v52 And all the gold of the offering that they offered up to the LORD, of the captains of thousands, and of the captains of hundreds, was sixteen thousand seven hundred and fifty shekels.
v53 (For the men of war had taken spoil, every man for himself.)
v54 And Moses and Eleazar the priest took the gold of the captains of thousands and of hundreds, and brought it into the tabernacle of the congregation, for a memorial for the children of Israel before the LORD. (KJV)

Taking Note: Numbers 31

v48 The army commanders went to Moses
v49 and said, " Sir, we have counted our troops, and not one soldier is missing.
(Contemporary English Version)

v50 So we want to give the LORD all the gold jewelry we took from the Midianites. It's our gift to him for watching over us and our troops."
v51 Moses and Eleazar accepted the jewelry from the commanders,
(Contemporary English Version)

v52 and its total weight was over four hundred pounds.
v53 This did not include the things that the soldiers had kept for themselves.
v54 So Moses and Eleazar placed the gold in the LORD's sacred tent to remind Israel of what had happened.
(Contemporary English Version)

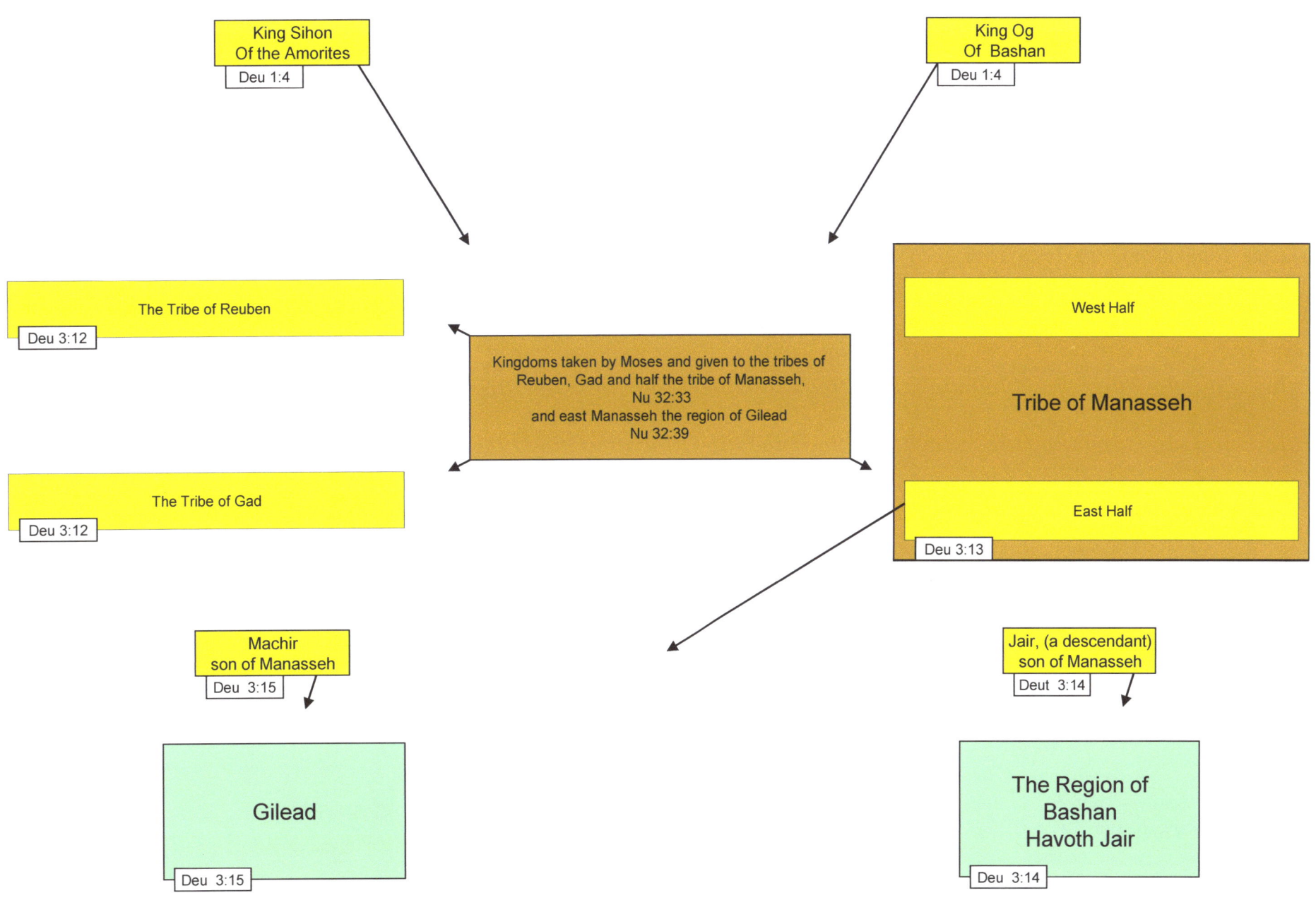

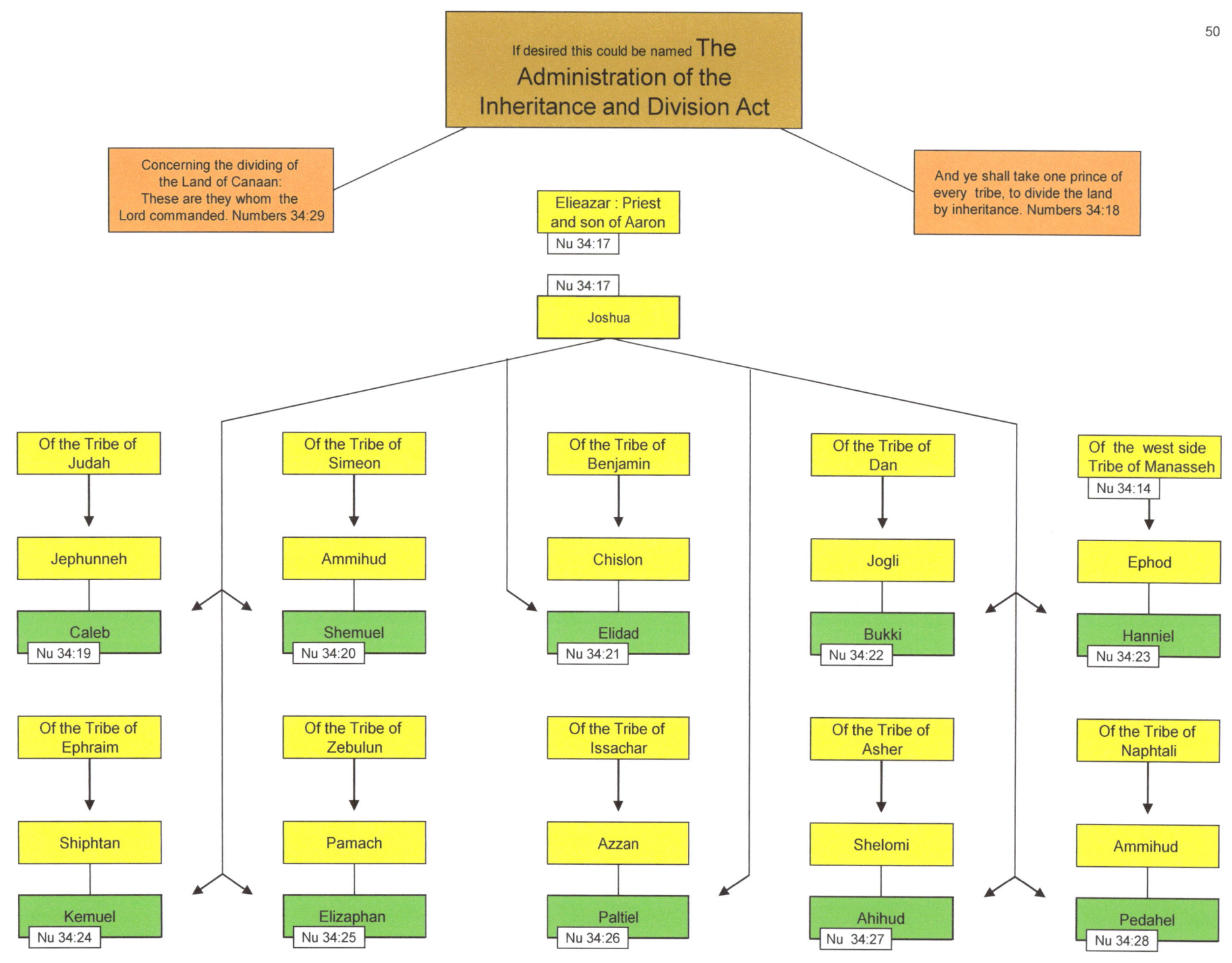

The Giants of Times Past

Deuteronomy 2nd Chapter

9 And the LORD said unto me, Distress not the Moabites, neither contend with them in battle: for I will not give thee of their land for a possession; because I have given Ar unto the children of Lot for a possession.

12 The Horims also dwelt in Seir beforetime; but the children of Esau succeeded them, when They had destroyed them from before them, and dwelt in their stead; as Israel did unto the land of his possession, which the LORD gave unto them.

19 And when thou comest nigh over against the children of Ammon, distress them not, nor meddle with them: for I will not give thee of the land of the children of Ammon any possession; because I have given it unto the children of Lot for a possession.

The Moabites to succeed

God speaks to Moses words of clarification before the crossing of the Jordan. Moses in turn speaks to the people of Israel the words spoken to him from God. In the first chapter of Deuteronomy, God demonstrates a fatherly type of self control in the face of what appeared to have been disappointment. God knew his children could have won, because he wouldn't have allowed them to fail. This is what he wanted them to understand.

The Children of Esau to succeed

God reminds Moses how it unfolded. He goes step by step. He reminds Moses of how he brought Israel out of Egypt, lead them with the cloud by day and fire at night and of his intent to keep his promise to Abraham, Isaac and Jacob. Then, it was time to fight and you turned away, because of the way it looked. So God tells of three different accounts of giants being displaced in times past. God could say, there was nothing new with what you were about to face.

The Ammonites to succeed

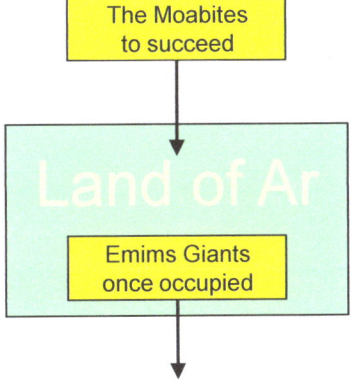

Land of Ar

Emims Giants once occupied

Land of Seir

Horim Giants once occupied

Deut. 1:8 Go in and possess the land

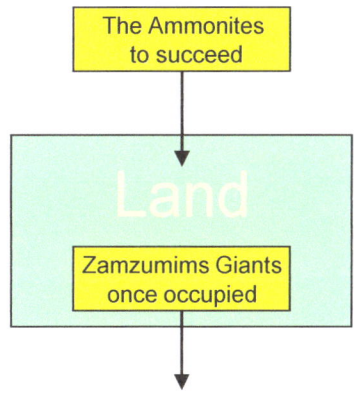

Land

Zamzumims Giants once occupied

Deuteronomy

Chapter 6
Observe God's laws that you may prosper. Write them down and tell your sons so that God can be a God to "you", as an individual and "you" as a people.

Chapter 7
God kept an oath he swore to Israel's forefathers. He stated, "Those who hate him he, will repay to their face by destruction. If we as adopted Israeli's follow God's command, decrees, and laws, the enemy will see God.

Chapter 8
Follow every command. Man lives on every word that comes from the mouth of God. He punishes those whom He loves. It is God that gives ability to produce wealth.

Chapter 9
Prepare to displace those that are greater than you because of their own wickedness. Although the people of Israel have been "stiff necked", Moses prayed that God would not destroy them and God did not.

Chapter 10
God remakes the ten commandments. The people are reminded to observe God's commandments for their own good. It was not God's will to destroy them.

Chapter 11
God reminds the people to keep the charge of God. The children has not seen God's hand against Egypt, but the older adults has. God will cause Israel's enemies to fear

Chapter 12
Instruction for new land concerning the wicked of that land, also concerning tithes, offerings & vows. Instructions also given to not eat blood & to not copy in offering up their sons and daughters as burnt offerings to gods.

Chapter 13
If a proven prophet tell you to leave God, do not listen. He shall be put to death. The same with close relatives and friends.

Belial

This name represents, along with their children and followers, someone who desires to see the separation between God and his people according to the reading in verses 12-16.

King James version
¹²If thou shalt hear say in one of thy cities, which the LORD thy God hath given thee to dwell there, saying, ¹³Certain men, the children of Belial, are gone out from among you, and have withdrawn the inhabitants of their city, ...

New International Verson
¹² If you hear it said about one of the towns the LORD your God is giving you to live in ¹³ that wicked men have arisen among you and have led the people of their town astray,…

2 Corinthians 6:15 KJV

And what concord hath Christ with Belial? or what part hath he that believeth with an infidel?

Christianity – "Belial is Satan, king of hell, Lord of arrogance."
The Ascension of Isaiah – "Belial is the angel of lawlessness."
The Dead Sea Scrolls – "Belial is the leader of the sons of darkness."
Testament of the Twelve Patriarchs – "God's opponent."

Chapter 14
Israel is a peculiar people and may not eat anything. They are instructed what is clean and what is not.

Chapter 15
Debts shall be forgiven every 7 years, slaves allowed to go free. Instruction to lend to other nation but not to borrow.

Chapter 16
Observe the month of Abib, the month Israel was bought out of Egypt and keep the "Passover".

Chapter 17
No evil favored or blemished scarifies permitted. Worshipping other gods, the sun, the moon, or any host of heaven in not permitted.

Chapter 18
The Levites are to eat the offering offered to the lord made by fire. Do not offer your sons and daughters to be burnt offerings.

Chapter 19
A city for the Innocent to be established in the event of an accident. No one is to be condemned on the bases of one witness. No one is to falsely witness against another.

Chapter 20
Israel to not be afraid of the large number of their enemies. God is the same God that brought them out of Egypt. He promises again to be with them in battle.

Chapter 21
If a man is found dead, the city nearest to the body is to perform a Godly duty. Mercy is to be sought and a Guilty charge to be avoided.

Chapter 22
- Neighborly behavior, neighborly expectations.
- Man should not wear that which pertains to a woman.
- A "thought to be" virgin wife and virgins of the city.

Chapter 23
- Who shall not enter into the congregation of the Lord.
- The Egyptians that were with Israel should not be despised and the 3rd generation of them can enter.

- There is to be no prostitutes or sodomy in the land of Israel and offerings given to the Lord from these earnings is an abomination.
- The word usury indicates interest on borrowed money and commodities. Usury should not be practiced between brothers in Israel.

Chapter 24
- A husband not to remarry his "put away" wife after her second marriage from another man ends.
- A father should pay for his wrongs, and a son for his.

Chapter 25
- The elders of the city to judge between right and wrong.
- Do not muzzle the ox that tread out the corn.
- A brother to build up his dead brother's name through the surviving sister-in-law.

Chapter 26
Isaac directed, then encouraged to wait on the promise. He becomes wealthy and intimidating. A covenant is made with Abimelech at Abimelech's request. He recognizes that God is with Isaac.

Chapter 26

Abimelech

The king of Philistines in Gerar Gen. 20:1,2

Phicol

Commands Abimelect's forces Gen. 21:22

Ahuzzath

Abimelech's personal advisor Gen. 26:26

Chapter 27
- After crossing over into Jordan, build an alter and offer a peace offering. Eat there and rejoice before the Lord.
- Curse be he that takes a reward to slay innocent blood.

Chapter 28
- The blessings of obedience.
- The curses of disobedience.

Chapter 29
- The words of the Covenant:
- The shoes on your feet have not worn out.
- The secret things belong unto the Lord our God.

Chapter 30
"...I have set before you life and death, blessing and cursing: therefore choose life that you and your seed may live."

Chapter 31
⁶Be strong and of a good courage, fear not, nor be afraid of them: for the LORD thy God, he it is that doth go with thee; he will not fail thee, nor forsake thee.

¹⁷Then my anger shall be kindled against them in that day, and I will forsake them, and I will hide my face from them, and they shall be devoured, and many evils and troubles shall befall them; so that they will say in that day, are not these evils come upon us, because our God is not among us?

Chapter 32

Jeshurun

v15 But Jeshurun waxed fat, and kicked: thou art waxen fat, thou art grown thick, thou art covered with fatness; then he forsook God which made him, and lightly esteemed the Rock of his salvation. KJV

God changed Jacob's name to Israel. Israel's descendants indeed is in the heart of God. The love and desire that God has for his people is so strong that it seems that God speaks poetically calling Jacob and Israel, Jeshurun. (see Isaiah 44:1-3 also Deut. 33:4,5 KJV)

Chapter 33
¹And this is the blessing, wherewith Moses the man of God blessed the children of Israel before his death.

Chapter 34
⁵So Moses the servant of the LORD died there in the land of Moab, according to the word of the LORD.
¹⁰And there arose not a prophet since in Israel like unto Moses, whom the LORD knew face to face,

Time From The Creation Of Adam

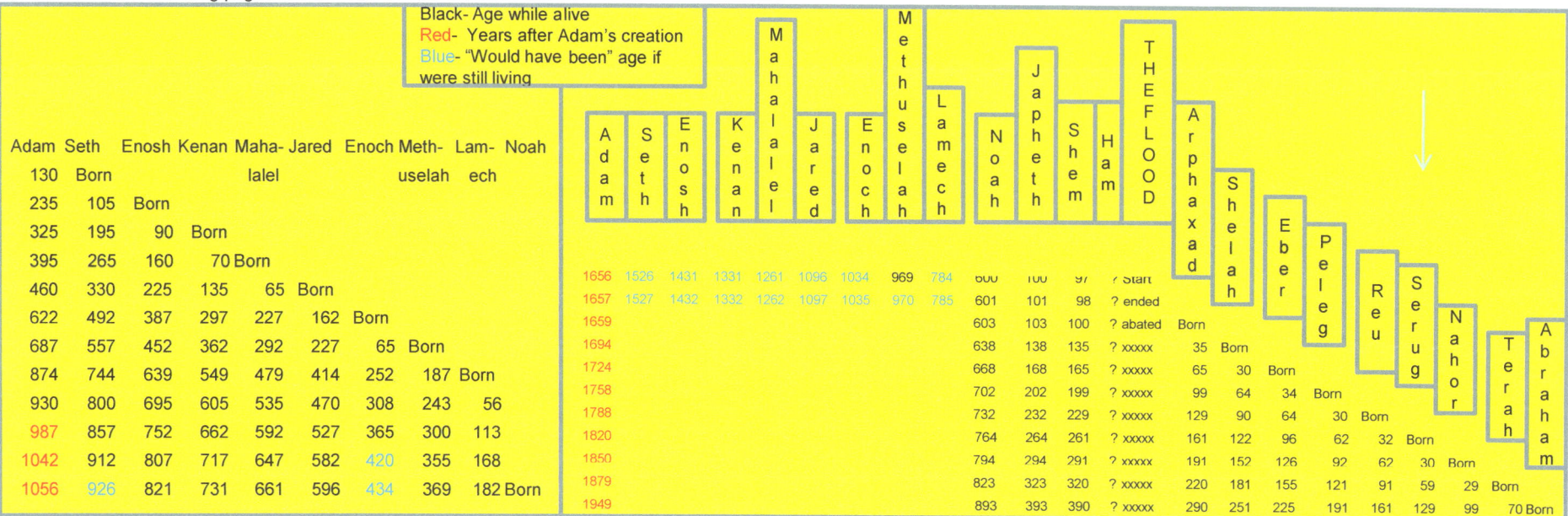

This chart gives what is given according to the Bible. It is so awesome when numbers add up and the picture becomes clearer. God is an artist, and an artist in more than one way. Do you ever get the thought that his desires are that, "the reaching to understand the truth in all situations would become common place?" That is the intent, isn't it: to understand what he gives to us and for us to live by it? And this has to be done with the present understanding that you now have going forward, receiving and changing according to what is given. To whom much is given, much is required. Again, this is done from the present level of faith. Which means, we have to sometimes seek one more tidbit of information to get a better understanding before you are allowed to say we have a complete understanding, if even then. In any case, seeking… is God approved.

When hunting here, as far as the chart is concerned, you have to do the math. Adam is the first man. When Adam was born and he took his first breath, he took it inside of the first year. On his first birthday, when he became a year old, that was the mark of one full year completed and the mark of the second new year starting. There was another significant "beginning marker" that's worth noting. God placed a marker on Israel's exit from Egypt and mandated that it be deemed as the first month of the year, which was called Abib, the first new month of the first new year for Israel.

According to the Bible, God did not place a calendar to mark the months and years of Adam's time period. But, with the numbers the Bible gives, it allows us to follow the years of his lifetime and beyond. This can be done from the time of his creation, to well past his death, allowing many individuals and certain event to be marked on a time line. I have called this the, "Adamic time Measurement", "The Adamic Year", "The Adam Year" and even the "Adam time chart". These terms represents a search for a name that depicts, measuring time from a consciously marked and recorded time beginning. This beginning is that of Adam and his descendants and their descendants. I think that Gen. 1:14 comes into play here.

"And God said, Let there be lights in the firmament of the heaven to divide the day from the night; and let them be for signs, and for seasons, and for days, and years:"

Noah was born in the Adamic year, or Adam year if you like, 1056. That is 1,056 years after the creation of Adam. We know the story of Noah. God was so upset with the whole world that he started over. The numbers show us the same picture that the words of the Bible tell. The world was lost except for Noah and his family. It even shows that Methuselah, at age 969 might have lived longer had it not been for the flood. Again, when Adam died at age 930, Noah was not yet born, his father was 56 and his grandfather Methuselah was 243. Noah died at the age of 950, 2006 years after the creation of Adam. He was the first of the Bible linage names given, to die over 2000 years after the creation of Adam. When Noah died, Adam had already been dead for 1,076 years. It may not sound like much, but it is still true. Noah's death marks the first of the ten names given in the generational line that has more than a 1,000 year spread between Adam's death and their death. The numbers show everyone on one side, except for Noah and his family which is shown, by the numbers, to be on the other. After the flood Noah is now the new "First Man" in the world. It is not by his own doing. And it is with Devine Hands and deep meaning that secures his position. The numbers confirm the written word.

The flood started in the Adamic year of 1656 and ended in the Adamic year of 1657. According to the Bible, Arphaxad was born two years after the flood and his father, Seth was 100. Maybe it is not appropriate to say that God did not give us a calendar. How was Moses able to write all of this. How did he have the insight of the six days of creation and the seventh day of rest. Well, the written word tell us that Moses talked with God face to face. Well, at the least Moses was face to face with a concentrated presence of God's essence and intellect. This is at God's desecration as to how much. Like a Christian feeling the spirit of God while home alone and having a good prayer, how strong the person feels God's presence is up to God. Without God's discretion in revealing his attendance, Moses would have died. But, God it seems, does show and trust Moses to an abnormally high degree of the revealing of his presence. God reminded Israel that no nation has ever had the presence of God in such a manner. He indicates their privileged position in being God's chosen people, even to the revealing of his historical work to a man who is one of them.

Helpful instructions to use the chart

How to determine the age of an individual's father at the time of the individual's birth.

See the person's name at the top of the chart. Go down until you see "born". This is when the person was born. The father's age will be to the immediate left most of the time.

How to determine age of an individual at the time of their death.

See person's name at the top of the chart. Go down to the only bold number in the column. That is the person age at time of death.

How to determine the number of years since the creation of Adam at the time of an individuals birth.

See the person's name at the top of the chart. Go down until you see "born". Look to the far left column under Adam. Black or red, this is the number of years since the creation of Adam at the time of an individual's birth.

How to determine the number of years since the creation of Adam at the time of an individual's death.

See the person's name at the top of the chart. Go down to the only bold number that represents the age at time of death. Look to the red column to the left under Adam. This is the number of years since the creation of Adam at the time of an individual's death.

How to determine how long Adam has been dead when an individual died.

See the person at the top of the chart. Go down to the only bold black number in that row. Look to the far left column under Adam. Subtract 930 from that number (Adam's age at time of his death). This is the number of years that Adam has been dead when the individual died.

How to determine the age of an individual at the time of Adam's death.

See the person's name at the top of the chart. Go down to the only bold black number. Look to the far left under Adam. Subtract 930 (Adam's age at time of his death) from that number. Take that sum and subtract it from the individual's age at time of death. (The only bold black number) This is their age when Adam died. Or you can do it the easy way, put you finger on 930 under Adam and slide it over. Applies only to 8 Patriarchs.

How to determine the time line of Adam's life and time since his creation.

This is determined from the numerical information the Bible itself gives. The best way to get this information is to read carefully from the beginning and write down the names and the numbers associated with each name. A consistent time line begins to appear. Eventually, correct math will be your only concern.

How to check the calculation of an individual's age at the time of death.

The scriptures tell the age, but you can still subtract the father's age at time of individual's birth from Adam's age, the red numbers to far left if after age 930. They will be black if 930 of before.

How to recheck the calculations of Adam's time line.

Make sure what you have written is what the Bible gives. Start with Adam's age of 130 at Seth's birth. This is the time since Adam's creation and also his age, simple. The next line is connected and motivated by Seth's age at the time of his son's birth, Enosh. Seth's age is also a continuation of Adam's age. Add the two (Adam's age and Seth' age). Enosh age is a Continuation of Adam's age and will be added in as well. The time line grows.

How to determine that the information you have is right compared to information you have found elsewhere.

Study for yourself. Intend to tell the truth and what the Bible says. Then tell the truth and what the Bible says. Recheck your findings.

Time Line According To Adam's Creation and Life

56

	A	B	C	D	E	F	G	H	I	J	K	L	M	N	O	P	Q	R	S
1	Adam	Seth	Enosh	Kenan	Mahalaleel	Jared	Enoch	Methusela	Lamech	Noah	Japhath	Sham	Ham	Flood	Arphaxad	Salah	Eber	Peleg	Reu
2	130	Born																	
3	235	105	Born																
4	325	195	90	Born															
5	395	265	160	70	Born														
6	460	330	225	135	65	Born													
7	622	492	387	297	227	162	Born												
8	687	557	452	362	292	227	65	Born											
9	874	744	639	549	479	414	252	187	Born										
10	930	800	695	605	535	470	308	243	56										
11	987	857	752	662	592	527	365	300	113										
12	1042	912	807	717	647	582	420	355	168										
13	1056	926	821	731	661	596	434	369	182	Born									
14	1140	1010	905	815	745	680	518	453	266	84									
15	1235	1105	1000	910	840	775	613	548	361	179									
16	1290	1160	1055	965	895	830	668	603	416	234									
17	1422	1292	1187	1097	1027	962	800	735	548	366									
18	1556	1426	1321	1231	1161	1096	934	869	682	500	Born								
19	1559	1429	1324	1234	1164	1099	937	872	685	503	3	Born	?						
20	1651	1521	1416	1326	1256	1191	1029	964	777	595	95	92	?						
21	1656	1526	1421	1331	1261	1096	1034	969	782	600	100	97	?	Start					
22	1657	1527	1422	1332	1262	1097	1035	970	783	601	101	98	?	1					
23	1659	1529	1424	1334	1264	1099	1037	972	785	603	103	100	?	2	Born				
24	1694	1564	1459	1369	1299	1134	1072	1007	820	638	138	135	?	37	35	Born			
25	1724	1594	1489	1399	1329	1164	1102	1037	850	668	168	165	?	67	65	30	Born		
26	1758	1628	1523	1433	1363	1198	1136	1071	884	702	202	199	?	101	99	64	34	Born	
27	1788	1658	1553	1463	1393	1228	1166	1101	914	732	232	229	?	131	129	94	64	30	Born
28	1820	1690	1585	1495	1425	1260	1198	1133	946	764	264	261	?	163	161	126	96	62	32

	A	B	C	D	E	F	G	H	I	J	K	L	M	N	O	P	Q	R	S
29	1850	1720	1615	1525	1455	1290	1228	1163	976	794	294	291	?	193	191	152	126	92	62
30	1879	1749	1644	1554	1484	1319	1257	1192	1005	823	323	320	?	222	220	181	155	121	91
31	1949	1869	1714	1624	1554	1389	1327	1262	1075	893	393	390	?	292	290	251	225	191	161
32	1959	1879	1724	1634	1564	1399	1337	1272	1085	903	403	400	?	302	300	261	235	201	171
33	1997	1917	1762	1672	1602	1437	1375	1310	1123	941	441	438	?	340	338	299	273	239	209
34	1998	1918	1763	1673	1603	1438	1376	1311	1124	942	442	439	?	341	339	300	274	240	210
35	2006	1916	1771	1681	1611	1446	1384	1319	1132	950	450	447	?	349	347	308	282	248	218
36	2010	1920	1775	1685	1615	1450	1388	1323	1136	954	454	451	?	353	351	312	286	252	222
37	2023	1933	1688	1608	1628	1453	1401	1346	1149	967	467	464	?	366	364	325	299	265	235
38	2024	1934	1689	1609	1629	1454	1402	1347	1150	968	468	465	?	367	365	326	300	266	236
39	2027	1937	1792	1702	1632	1457	1405	1340	1153	971	471	468	?	370	368	329	303	269	239
40	2034	1944	1799	1709	1639	1464	1412	1347	1160	978	478	475	?	377	375	336	310	276	246
41	2035	1945	1800	1710	1640	1465	1413	1348	1161	979	479	476	?	378	376	337	311	277	247
42	2048	1958	1813	1723	1653	1478	1426	1361	1174	992	492	489	?	391	389	350	324	290	260
43	2049	1959	1814	1724	1654	1479	1427	1362	1175	993	493	490	?	392	390	351	325	291	261
44	2050	1960	1815	1725	1655	1480	1428	1363	1176	994	494	491	?	393	391	352	326	292	262
45	2084	1994	1849	1759	1689	1514	1462	1397	1210	1028	528	525	?	427	425	386	360	326	296
46	2086	1996	1851	1761	1691	1516	1464	1399	1212	1030	530	525	?	429	427	388	362	328	298
47	2089	1999	1854	1764	1694	1519	1467	1402	1215	1033	533	560	?	432	430	391	365	331	301
48	2097	2007	1862	1772	1723	1527	1475	1410	1223	1041	541	538	?	440	438	399	373	339	309
49	2109	2019	1874	1784	1735	1539	1487	1422	1235	1053	553	550	?	452	450	411	385	351	321
50	2124	2034	1889	1799	1750	1554	1502	1437	1250	1068	568	565	?	467	465	426	400	366	336
51	2131	2044	1896	1806	1757	1561	1509	1444	1257	1075	575	572	?	474	472	433	407	373	743
52	2149	2062	1914	1824	1775	1579	1527	1462	1275	1093	593	590	?	492	490	451	425	391	761
53	2159	2072	1924	1834	1785	1589	1537	1472	1285	1103	603	600	?	502	500	461	435	401	371
54	2172	2085	1937	1847	1795	1602	1550	1485	1298	1116	616	613	?	515	513	474	448	414	384
55	2188	2101	1953	1863	1811	1618	1566	1501	1314	1132	632	629	?	531	529	490	464	430	400
56	2229	2142	1994	1904	1852	1659	1607	1542	1355	1173	673	670	?	572	570	531	505	471	441
57	2256	2169	2021	1931	1879	1686	1634	1569	1382	1200		697		599	597	558	532	498	468

		T	U	V	W	X	Y	Z	AA	AB	AC	AD	AE	AF	AG	AH	AI	AJ	AK	AL
		Serug	Nahor	Terah	Abraham	Sarah	Ismael	Isaac	Esau	Jacob	Levi									
28		Born																		
29		30	Born																	
30		59	29	Born																
31		129	99	70	Born															
32		139	109	80	10	Born														
33		177	147	118	48	38														
34		178	148	119	49	39														
35		186	156	127	57	47														
36		190	160	131	61	51														
37		203	173	144	74	64														
38		204	174	145	75	65														
39		207	177	148	78	68														
40		214	184	155	85	75														
41		215	185	156	86	76	Born													
42		228	198	169	99	89	13													
43		229	199	170	100	90	14	Born												
44		230	200	171	101	91	15	1												
45		264	234	205	135	125	49	35												
46		266	236	207	137	127	51	37												
47		269	239	210	140	131	54	40												
48		277	247	218	148	139	62	48												
49		289	259	230	160	151	74	60	Born	Born										
50		294	274	245	175	166	89	75	15	15										
51		301	281	252	182	173	96	82	22	22										
52		319	299	270	200	191	114	100	40	40										
53		339	309	280	210	201	124	110	50	50	Born-3 ?									
54		352	322	293	223	214	137	123	63	63	10-13?									
55		368	338	309	239	230	153	139	79	79	26-29?									58

	T	U	V	W	X	Y	Z	AA	AB	AC	AD	AE	AF	AG	AH	AI	AJ	AK	AL
	Serug	Nahor	Terah	Abraham	Sarah	Ismael	Isaac	Esau	Jacob	Levi	AD	AE	AF	AG	AH	AI	AJ	AK	AL
56	409	379	350	280	271	194	180	120	120	67-70?									
57	436	406	377	307	298	221	207		147	94-97?									
58	19	20	21	22	23	24	25	26	27	28									
59	230	148	205	175	127	137	180	UN-KNOWN	147	137									
60	NL	NL	NL	NL	NL	NL	NL	NL	NL	NL									
61	-1120	-1068	-1154	-1194	-1155	-1242	-1299	UN-KNOWN	-1326	?									
62	677	646	621	598	Not averaged in	575	556	UN-KNOWN	537	520									
63	10853	11001	11206	11381	11508	11645	11825	UN-KNOWN	11972	12109									
64	2050	1998	2084	2124	2085	2172	2229	UN-KNOWN	2256	?									
65	109	104	102	102	101	UN-KNOWN	100	UN-KNOWN	UN-KNOWN	UN-KNOWN									
66																			
67																			
68																			
69																			
70																			
71																			
72																			
73																			
74																			
75																			
76																			
77																			
78																			
79																			
80																			
81																			
82																			
83																			

	A	B	C	D	E	F	G	H	I	J	K	L	M	N	O	P	Q	R	S
	Adam	Seth	Enosh	Kenan	Mahalaleel	Jared	Enoch	Methusela	Lamech	Noah	Japhath	Sham	Ham	Flood	Arphaxad	Salah	Eber	Peleg	Reu
58	1	2	3	4	5	6	7	8	9	10	11	12	13		14	15	16	17	18
59	930	912	905	910	895	962	365	969	777	950	UN-KNOWN	600	UN-KNOWN	1 YR 10 d	438	433	464	239	239
60	930	800	695	605	535	470	308	243	56	NL	NL	NL	NL	NL	NL	NL	NL	NL	NL
61	0	-112	-210	-305	-360	-492	-57	-726	-721	-1076	UN-KNOWN	-1229	UN-KNOWN	-727	-1167	-1196	-1258	-1067	-1097
62	930	921	916	914	910	919	no death	926	908	912	UN-KNOWN	881	UN-KNOWN	no death	841	806	780	742	708
63	930	1842	2747	3657	4552	5514	no death	6483	7260	8210	UN-KNOWN	8810	UN-KNOWN	N/A	9248	9681	10145	10384	10623
64	0	1042	1140	1235	1290	1422	987	1656	1651	2006	UN-KNOWN	2159	UN-KNOWN	1657	2097	2131	2188	1997	2027
65	130	118	108	99	92	104	98	109	103	156	No Rec.	151	No Rec.	N/A	141	132	125	119	114
66																			
67																			
68																			
69																			
70																			
71																			
72																			
73																			
74																			
75																			
76																			
77																			
78																			
79																			
80																			
81																			
82																			
83																			
84																			
85																			60

The Adam time line is a direct result of the information given by the Bible. Understanding and feeling confident about what the Bible says from chapter one verse one will only help you increase in knowledge as you continue to read and study. You never want to be argumentative by any means. You do want to be able to know when you hear wrong information, and there is plenty of that to be heard. God has the desire that you have an understanding, and surely, a better understanding when the opportunity presents itself. God gave us his word; therefore, we have the opportunity to increase understanding for ourselves. Read the Bible. Read it with the desire to grasp what the whole letter is saying. When a sincere heart sincerely searches for the truth, then... well, let the Bible speak for itself. James 4:8, "Draw near to God and He will draw near to you". And what about Matt 7:7, "... seek, and ye shall find....". If you do this, you may start to have inclinations concerning the next spiritual chapter that God is writing, and maybe even know what is to come next on the world stage. I'm just saying. The Bible is the foundation. It is a serious rock with an attraction. It has a universal and gravitational pull. If this were not the case then the, "would be hell on earth", might not be equal to that of hell itself, but those "would be citizens" probably would think, "Surely, hell can not be any worse than this."

Concerning this chart, row 1 column A is Adam having been created. That is the event in that row. The event in row two is the birth of Seth and that happened at the Adam age or the Adamic year of 130. The numbers in black represent Adam still alive. The event in row 10 is Adam's death. He was 930. The day of his creation and his physical death has been and will continue to be markers. The numbers in red continue to represent Adam's life as if he were still alive although he is now dead.

Sometimes, when discovering something new for yourself, you might have the audacity, for a brief second, to think that no one knows this, but you. Then, reality hit and that bubble quickly bursts. Well, here is one of those times. Look at row 11 column G. Gen. 5:24 "And Enoch walked with God: and he was not; for God took him." To make it clear, Enoch pleased God. Enoch is the 7th person in this generation line that the Bible names. God, consciously and knowingly, takes him at the age of 365; 7 days in a week, 365 days in a year. Wouldn't you say those are markers? Well, if you're thinking "no big deal", look at row 11 again. He is the first of those named to be taken/die after the death of Adam. That is a notable point. Because, it seems that Adam's birth (creation) and death are not only markers where spans of time can be measured, but also can show, it seems, others whom God himself has placed in a certain position, and it may even show... on whom God has placed honor. Here again is the example of Noah. Look at J13, he is the first of those named, Noah is, to be born 1000 years after the creation of Adam. Adam is the marker. Look at J35. Noah is the first of those named, to die over 2000 years after the creation of Adam. Adam is the marker. Look at J61. Again, Noah is in a first category. This time, he is the first of those named to die after Adam has been dead for over a 1000 years. Again, Adam is the marker. But, Noah is the honored subject in relation to the named marker, which is Adam. Adam's time line show the position of Noah compared to the other patriarchs. There are two things that separate Noah from those that came before him; allow me to give the second one first which is, "The Flood". All those before him were on one side and Noah on the other. Sure, they all arrived before the flood, including Noah, but Noah is the only one that ended up on the other side. They are all gone. Noah is now the Presiding figure; the new face and representation of a brand new beginning. Now, that is an honored man who has an honorable position, don't you think? It is especially honorable, when that position has been appointed and placed on you by God himself. And the first thing that separated Noah; a couple of days. Yes, a couple of days or so, separated Noah from the rest. 2 Peter 3:8, "But do not forget this one thing, dear friends: With the Lord a day is like a thousand years, and a thousand years are like a day." When teaching the word of God, it does not have to be stretched or forced. God gives his message, and he knows how to watch over his word. Concerning the couple of days separating Noah and those that were named before him, lets look at those years in the context of 1000 years being like a day.

Ready? One day at midnight, (Adam time line starts with him) Adam was created on this early morning. Along with Adam, there were eight others who arrived naturally by birth this same day, nine in all. The 1st and same day of Adam's creation, he died at 10:32 pm. At 11:41 p.m. that same night, it was confirmed that a miracle had taken place and Enoch, someone whom God honored, was taken. Enoch was Adam's great, great, great, great grandson. Just an hour or so later into the early morning hours of the next and 2nd day, Adam's son Seth, also dies. On this second day, Noah was born and the remaining six of the original nine dies. A new day comes; the third day. Noah, the only one of the ten to see this day, dies shortly after midnight, on the third day.

Here is another marker that can't be ignored, if you believe in the markers at all. Look at L58. Shem is number 12 to be named according to birth order in the generational line. Jesus comes through the bloodline of Shem. For that matter, Jesus comes through the blood line of one of the 12 sons of Jacob. God changed Jacob's name to Israel. Israel's 12 sons become the fathers of the 12 tribes of Israel: the people who later become the nation of Israel. Oh, did I mention there are 12 months in a year. If this, indeed is a principle thing with God, then it looks as though Shem is positioned and honored also, and rightfully so. We go by the 12 month Gregorian Calendar today. However, the twelve month calendar is not just a modern day thing. It started with God handing down to Moses a new 12 month Calendar on the exiting of Egypt starting with the month of Abib , Exodus 13:4. The first month was also noted being called Nisan, Nehemiah 2:1. Deuteronomy 1:3 show Moses speaks to the people in the eleventh month. The 12 month Jewish calendar is 1. Nisan, 2 Lyar, 3.Sivan, 4. Tammuz, 5. Av, 6. Elul, 7. Tishrei, 8. Mar, 9. Kislev, 10. Tevet, 11. Shevat, 12. Adar. If God himself orchestrated and honored the life of some of the Patriarchs to be markers for measuring and keeping time, then wouldn't Jesus' life surely be a marker? And what kind of marker would his life be? Jesus is greater than Adam, Enoch, Noah Shem and Moses. And so is His marker.

Who doubts that time stands on the shoulder of Jesus? Well, there are those who will openly display their reservation. But, like Adam, except greater , Jesus' death and birth are forever engraved as navigational points of time. The markers that Jesus' life and death represents, gives credence to the hypothesis that markers (you may call them what you like) are indeed, principle elements of, and a way of functioning in, the mind and heart of God. This was demonstrated in a small way, one might say, with Moses in Exodus 13:4. But, it was well established with Adam, Enoch, and Sham.

I would like to paint a picture; a non-elaborate picture. Ready? God makes a world. He then establishes the days and the weeks; the months and the years. He determines the north, south, east, and west directions. Then, well maybe before then, he launches time, which is in fact, intricate work that belongs in the class of awesomeness. It is more than time starting from zero and just counting on into infinity. Hypothetically, the segments of time; days, months, years and even weeks are marked by the early patriarchs. And he caused it to be established and kept by 'the heavens". The continuation of time from a single point going forward is noted by Jesus Christ himself, so much so that time is even measured going backwards from his birth by what we call "BC", which literally means, "Before Christ". It is so well instituted that no man or woman who does not like it, can change it. God made this world and prepared it for us. He set the parameters where by we can navigate in it. For the sake of explanation, lets call this world a maze. Well, some men come along in this maze and lives his life in this maze, works and sleep in this maze, and do it all in the 24 hour days that God has established. While doing so, this man starts his own crusade to declare that God is not real. It is kind of a mind bender.

Here is one more that is inspiring. Look at A31. The event in that row is W31. This would not be as big of a deal except for the fact that it's Abram, whose name was changed to Abraham. He was born in the Adamic year in 1949. The "Israel" that we know today, which was promised to that same Abraham, declared independence and became a nation again in 1948 AD. This same modern day Israel was admitted as a member of the United Nations by majority vote on May 11,1949 AD.

Line 58 simply numbers each generation from Adam on, according to birth.

Line 59 is the age at time of death for the named person.

Line 60 is the age at time of death for the named person minus the time span in years between their death and Adam's death.

Line 61 is the calculated time span, in years between the individual's death and Adam's death. This is the number you subtract from line 59 to get line 60.

Line 62 is the average age at the time of death, adding one person at a time. *

Line 63 adds each age together, at time of death, one at a time.

Line 64 is the Adamic Year in which the named person died and flood ended.

Line 65 is an average age at the time of first child being birth. **

*   Adam by himself makes the average age 930 years old. Adding his son Seth, who died at age 912, makes the average age 921 years old and so on. Although Noah is the tenth person to be named, his death makes the ninth averaged in, due to the fact that the Bible states that Enoch did not die, but God took him. What is worth noting here is that up to and including Noah, the average age at death stays in the 900's. There is no time of death noted for Japhath who would have been next, nor is there one noted for Ham, who is after Shem because there are no recorded deaths for either (Gen. 10:21 KJV, AMP, NKJV, NIV). So, Shem's death is recorded next and the average age at time of death adjusts to the 800's; 881 to be exact for Shem. There are few who doubts that the number 8 means, "a new beginning". Again, Jesus comes out of the bloodline of Shem. What is also worth noting here, with Adam being the first, is that there are nine 9's up to and again, including Noah. Please forgive me but, yes I have to say it. 9x9 is 81 which is on the back of the newly adjusted number 8, which falls on Shem, whose blood line carries Jesus. With Sham being the first, there are three 8's. 3x8, even the 24 hour day is covered. Then there are three 7's, three 6's, and with Abraham being the first, there are five 5's.

I like using the word "hypothesis" or "hypothesize", many times when I am trying to be humorous. But, I think it's a good word for when you are legitimately looking for understanding without arterial motives. The truth is what it is whether it helps your cause or not. Based on the information you have, you try to formulate a theory that could be true. Again, when you are honest, and you don't care where the truth is, you will be thrilled, not only knowing where, but what it is. Also, when seeking the truth, God knows, that is the reason that you are seeking, because you, at this moment, don't know what it is now. So, when you hypothesize out of your pure intention, you are doing what the Bible says, seeking, which is God approved. Your hypothesis is honorable before God. Now, it is possible that you could still be wrong. But, golden is your search when it is sincere and it pleases God. Not only that, a true search can only increase your understanding.

Now, having put forth that disclaimer, allow me to hypothesize sincerely, concerning the first nine, and Noah is certainly not excluded. They had a relationship with God that was greater than any human being on the planet today. Hear me out (This excludes the angels that the Bible talks about who may be among us). Now, keep in mind Lucifer was in heaven and seen things that you and I have never seen, well most of us anyway, who knows what God is showing some man or woman today. Lucifer had a relationship with God that most preachers and Christians or anyone who believes in God, would love to attain, but without the bad heart. It seems that the status of an individual's heart is more of a weighty matter than their spiritual encounters. It also looks like it is safe to say that spiritual encounters then, at that time, were totally on a different level. If that is true, then spiritual encounters, or the lack thereof, are not the issue. Sure, they're great to have, but not the issue. Adam and Eve had many encounters. Cain, who took his brother's life, had many encounters. Enoch, it stands to reason, had many encounters. No doubt the encounters were more than the Bible took the time to tell. If it is true that encounters are less frequent today or at the least, not in the same arena as then, that consequently says, that something has changed, and yet something has never changed. If a man's heart or even a spiritual being, I guess I would have to say, were to be God ward and be that wholesomely, then God himself judges the heart as to whether that be true. God, being who he is, judged Lucifer's heart as well as his thinking, which came out of his heart (Isaiah 14). That in sequence, produced behavior. Look at the encounters he had. Not only him, but look at the encounters that one third of the angels that followed him had, if indeed the understanding of Rev. 12 is accurate . What has changed are the encounters themselves, maybe. You may think we need them as to help increase people's faith. But, read on.

I had a notion (hypothesis) some years ago, and it was this. A man can experience a spiritual event so… "off the chain", or "mind blowing", to the point that it is not a matter if it happened or not, but whether he can tell it or not so that people will believe him. Well, the hypothesis goes on to say that it is possible for that same man to be under a tree, years later, doing drugs telling his friends about that experience. If indeed his heart had changed, then more than likely he would not be under the tree. Either way, the event itself is so fascinating, it's an encounter worth telling. Encounters then, could have been like ripe navel oranges on a large, unpicked, fruitful, naval orange tree. Today, it may or may not be that way, and maybe from God's point of view, it actually needs not to be that way. Why? Because one thing that has never changed and will never change is that God wants a pure and clean heart that is God ward. He wants it from human beings, and for that matter, from spiritual beings also; a simple requirement for all those that say they are with him. From before time began until now, the heart has been a big issue. It is the issue.

**   At the present time, I see no significance in these figures, other than the fact that the average age ends up to be 100 on Isaac, who is not the first born of Abraham, but is the first born to Abraham and Sarah together, to whom the promise was made. Abraham was 99 when he and Ishmael were circumcised. It was one year later and at age 100 when he received the promise with Isaac. Sometimes just looking and searching is exciting. It's God approved.

*   Continuing from line 62, the three number 7's equals 21. I have heard often in church that 21 is the number of "victory". As far as the five number 5's, which is 5 squared and equals 25, I have always heard the number 5 is for "grace". It does make sense to me, being that; 1. God promised Canaan (Israel) to Abraham and it turns out that the Jews of Israel rejected Jesus. But God made a promise and his grace will be sufficient. 2. To this day Israel does not rest on the entire land that God has desired for them to have. It has to be a lack of following instructions, but again, God made a promise and his grace has to be sufficient. If there is no grace for Israel, then there is no help. If there is no help then the promise would not be kept. Symbolically speaking, grace is needed in double portions in order for God to do what he wants here. With Abraham being first, to whom the promise was given, there are five 5's.

What I want to focus on are the three number 6's. I think this is amazing. 3x6 equals 18 and I feel like that means something. Well, how far can that go? What I feel has to be pushed aside because, like a good detective, you want the facts. You want to make your own judgments. Ok, let's give the facts.

Fact number one; Noah winds up being the new leader of the eight people populated world after the flood. I think it is safe to say, that he is the liaison between God and those who survived. Again, the numbers support the words that are spoken. I am sure you already noticed that all of the supporting numbers end in six, which is the first fact to be pointed out. If you did not notice, here they are again:

    first of the ten patriarchs to be born 1000 years after the creation of Adam, ... 1056 to be exact;
    first of the ten patriarchs to die 2000 years after the creation of Adam, ... 2006 to be exact;
    first of the ten patriarchs to die after Adam has already been dead for an 1000 years, ... 1076 to be exact.

I guess some would think that the devil has something to do with this. I read a scripture one time that reshaped my thinking. Read Psalms 18:1-11

    "... He made darkness his secret place...". That scripture is talking about God. Read Exodus 20:21

    " And the people stood afar off, and Moses drew near unto the thick darkness where God was."

After reading that, I realized that God owns the day and he owns the night. Some try to use the night for evil, but God never meant for the night to be a covering for wrong or evil in any way. Just like darkness is not evil, in and of itself, the number six or the number 666, is not an evil number, nor is it "God appointed" to be a representation thereof. Read John 3:19

    "And this is the condemnation, that light is come into the world and men loved darkness rather than light, because their deeds were evil."

When a number embodies a negative event such as "911" or takes on the persona of evil personified, it is true that it is hard to separate it in your thinking. I think if numbers had feelings, I would try to console the number six and say, "Sorry for the bad reputation you are getting, it's not your fault." Imagine you come home and wag your finger at a hammer and say, "Bad hammer, bad hammer", when the hammer, if it could talk, would respond and say, "Hey, you left me on the porch and that "Dennis the Menace" kid next door found me and went on a rampage." But, on to the point that I really want to make.

Fact number two; Noah is a multiplier. But that's is only part of it. The other part is that he came between the first set of three deaths of Adam, Enoch and Seth. Then he, Moses, was born, followed by the deaths of the remaining six, who were Enosh, Kenan, Mahalaleel, Jared, Methuselah, Lamech. Now, let's look at this for a second. No person on the planet, in a manner of speaking, can reject the idea that Adam is, "Somebody", in the eyes of God and man. When it comes to Enoch, of the two men, who is greater, Adam or Enoch? If you wanted to have a friendly and brotherly debate about it, yes I would love to be a quiet one in the room listening to both points of view. They both are seriously great men, but Enoch did please God, so much so, that God said, "Ahhh, just come on up". And finally, Seth, who is he that he can stand with men on a level such as this. Sure, theologians and Bible lovers know him today. But, I can see in my mind, way back when, someone saying, "Why is he here, and what is his name?" Someone #2 responds and says, "O That's Mr. Seth, of the three sons of Adam mentioned, he is the vessel that carries the bloodline to Jesus. Seth is an example of God intervening and making a way when it seems like man has made a mess of things. Able can not carry the blood line because Cain, his brother killed him. Cain can not do it now, because he has been cursed and called a vagabond, Gen 4:12. God's will continues, Seth is born,

Fact number three is that fact number one and two both exist. The one condones the other, as well as support and give credence to the idea about the other. Let me explain this way.

There is a scientist who has been looking for certain information for years. He still has not found it, but because of his search, he has come into a new understanding that conclusively, allows him to know where the information is. He still cannot get to it, don't know what it says or how large or small it is. But today, it's okay. He found out where it is. Yes, he will want more answers tomorrow, but today is a day of a small discovery and a little bit of satisfaction to go with it.

Here is a more appropriate example. There is a heavenly ceremony preparing to start. And you can believe there is order in the house. Positions are awarded by God himself. Seats of honor are well noted. Although, some are greater who are in attendance and some that are not as great, there are three seats that are well in mind. Not anyone can sit in them. And while all to be understood, is not completely understood by everyone in attendance because, it has not been revealed yet; even so, everyone is reverently and vastly in place.

In addition, I would like to offer one more thing. Numbers do not have a mindful agenda. You could say that they are like door knobs; inanimate objects... dead. But, when it comes to opening doors to a better understanding, they are extremely useful, and that for sure, is an understatement. Speaking of the number 6 and more specifically 666; it does not belong to Satan the way our minds have conjured. Intentionally or not, one of the attributes about Satan is that he likes to steal; to take as though it really belongs to him, whatever the item may be.

It is also a Biblical fact, that being in a certain position has been a priority of his heart. Although, numbers can not bring life to the "Word of God" because the Word of God is life all by itself, numbers can bring an agreement and help bring understanding to that which is already true, and that they do. I could even say, that numbers may not have a life of their own, but they do praise the Word of God. I do not know what the number 18 means. I do know it is the sum of 6+6+6 or better yet, 3x6, as equation-ally, spelled out by the patriots themselves. These are also facts that the detective wants to know. It stands to reason, that there have been carnal ones who have used the number 666 to participate in ungodly activities, that they were not in full spiritual understanding of. Likewise, one could imagine, that there are still spiritual foes of God, desiring to operate under the same banner as well, because of what the spiritual beings themselves understand it to mean, and because of what value "666" holds or represents in their heart. Another attribute of Satan is, after taking something that is not his, he corrupts it. What might be a deeper meaning of what is now a symbol "666" or the number 18, could be to Lucifer, a representation of a ceremonial position. But, as Satan, it has become like a much wanted, but unreachable, lustful desire. Reading the Pentateuch is like having God's invitation to a better understanding that leads, eventually, to the table of complete understanding.

#	Year	Diff
1	0	
2	130	130
3	235	105
4	325	90
5	395	70
6	460	65
7	622	162
8	687	65
9	874	187
10	930	56
11	987	57
12	1042	55
13	1056	14
14	1140	84
15	1235	95
16	1290	55
17	1422	132
18	1556	134
19	1559	3
20	1651	92
21	1656	5
22	1657	1
23	1659	2
24	1694	35
25	1724	30
26	1758	34
27	1788	30
28	1820	32
29	1850	30
30	1879	29
31	1949	70
32	1959	10
33	1997	38
34	1998	1
35	2006	8
36	2010	4
37	2023	13
38	2024	1
39	2027	3
40	2034	7
41	2035	1
42	2048	13
43	2049	1
44	2050	1
45	2084	34
46	2086	2
47	2089	3
48	2097	8
49	2109	2
50	2124	15
51	2131	7
52	2149	18
53	2159	10
54	2172	217
55	2188	16
56	2229	41
57	2256	27
58	1	2

The heart of God is rich with substance that can make a man spiritually complete. It will make him fulfilled also. There is satisfaction in completing instructions given by God. But, lets discuss attitudes. There are two types of, "I don't care", attitudes that could be concidered. One, is where an individual is wrecking their own life and the lives of people around them. Also, the person is being given life correcting instructions but, refuses to hear and displays a demeanor that says, "I don't care" . The other is, where someone cherishes when God simply, whispers in their direction a word of enlightenment. It can, at times, be an emotional occasion. Because, with obedience to each instruction given, it is viewed as fulfillment that will be gained and added to, the life that is already given. When a man has done everything he can do, according to what he believes that the heart of God has instructed, then he could say to himself, concerning the thoughts and opinions of others, "I don't care".

Do you think that the Bible contains all the contents of God's heart? One thing the Bible does do, is point you to his heart. And along with getting straight, black and white answers on a given subject, the Bible, as you continue to study, starts to paint a picture of his thinking process, which comes from his heart. Let me try this way. Here is an instruction that we read in the Bible that God is saying to his people in Amos 5:14;

"Seek good, not evil, that you may live… ." KJV

And the heart of God is revealed by his own words in Jeremiah 29:11;

"For I know the thoughts that I think toward you, says the Lord, thoughts of peace and not of evil to give you a future and a hope." NKJV

The Pentateuch, which is the first five books of the Bible, could be seen as the first few paragraphs of a long letter where God desires to be lovingly cordial, and intends to convey an atmosphere of conversation and openness. Again, it is like God is inviting his people to the table where he is looking forward to imparting thoughts that are for family, and friends of the family. But, you have to want to be apart of the fellowship.

The intent of this book, along with listing every name, is to help in studying the Bible, the Pentateuch in particular. The numbers in gray are the same numbers from the chart and counts in order, the events that are being taken noted, on the Adams time line. In your study, you may take note of an event that can be placed in the chart as well. The numbers in the middle, again are the same number from the chart, which is the Adam's time line. The third set of numbers, which is not on the chart, are the number of years between or from the prior event. For example, look at numbers 21 and 22 in grey. I would like to use this to show how this information came into understanding. Because, the Bible has supplied the scriptures that gives the numbers, we are able to safely calculate up to the flood, which is 1,656 years after the creation of Adam, also called the Adamic year 1656. Genesis 7:6 says,

"And Noah was six hundred years old when the flood of waters was upon the earth."

Genesis 8:13 says,

"And it came to pass in the six hundredth and first year, in the first month, the first day of the month, the waters were dried up from off the earth: and Noah removed the covering of the ark, and looked, and, behold, the face of the ground was dry."

This means, it was one year and some days. This was confirmed with the amplified version. There, in Genesis 8:18, it says,

"And Noah went forth, and his wife and his sons and their wives with him [after being in the ark one year and ten days]" Amplified Version

The prior event, which was in 1651 and five years earlier, was Lamech's death. The next event after the start of the flood is the end of the flood , one year later in 1657. Number 1 in gray shows the number zero. Zero represents the very moment that Adam was created. One year later, from the day of his creation, he had his first birthday. We can see the event that is mentioned next, and that is the birth of his son Seth, 130 years from the day of his creation. Enjoy.

Aaron	Page 21, 32-34	Aran -son of Duke Dishan a Horite	Page 13	Caleb	Page 29, 50
Abel	Page 3	Ard	Page 19	Canaan	Page 4-5
Abiasaph -son of Korah	Page 21	Areli	Page 18, 38	Caphtorim	Page 4
Abidah	Page 8	Arioch -king	Page 9	Carmi	Page 16, 36
Abidan	Page 24, 34	Ark-ite	Page 5	Casluhim	Page 4
Abihu	Page 21	Arodi	Page 18, 38	Chedorlaomer -king	Page 9
Abimael	Page 6	Arphaxad	Page 6	Cheran	Page 13
Abimelech	Page 53	Arvad-ite	Page 5	Chesed or Kesed	Page 7
Abiram	Page 32, 36	Asenath -wife	Page 18	Chislon	Page 50
Abraham	Page 7-10	Ashbel	Page 19, 44	Cozbi -daughter	Page 33
Achbor -father of king Baalhanan	Page 14	Ashenath - wife and daughter	Page 15	Cush	Page 4
Adah -Hittite daughter	Page 11	Asher	Page 15, 18, 46	Dan	Page 15, 19, 45
Adah -wife of Esau	Page 11	Ashkenaz	Page 4	Dathan	Page 32, 36
Adah -wife of Lamech	Page 3	Asriel	Page 42	Deborah -nurse	Page 11
Adam	Page 3	Asshurim	Page 8	Dedan	Page 4, 8
Adbeel	Page 8	Assir	Page 21	Deuel	Page 23
Ahiezer -son of Ammishaddai	Page 25	Assur	Page 6	Diklah	Page 6
Ahihud	Page 50	Azzan	Page 50	Dina -Daughter	Page 15
Ahiman	Page 31	Balaam	Page 33	Dishan -Duke	Page 13
Ahira -son of Enan	Page 25, 34	Balak	Page 33	Dishon -son of Anah	Page 13
Ahiram	Page 44	Balial	Page 52	Dodanim	Page 4
Ahisamach	Page 22	Baal Hanan -king	Page 14	Dumah	Page 8
Aholibamah -wife and daughter	Page 11, 13	Bara -king	Page 9	Ebal	Page 13
Ahuzzath	Page 53	Basemath	Page 11, 12	Eber	Page 6
Ajah -son of Duke Zibeon a Horite	Page 13	Becher	Page 43	Ehi	Page 19
Akan -son of Duke Ezer a Horite	Page 13	Becher -son of Benjamin	Page 19	Elam	Page 6
Almodad	Page 6	Becher -son of Eran	Page 43	Eldaah	Page 8
Alvan	Page 13	Bedad -father of king Hadad	Page 14	Eldad	Page 28
Amalek -Duke	Page 11	Beeri -Hittite	Page 11	Eleazar	Page 21, 27, 33
Amiel	Page 30	Bela -son of Benjaman	Page 19, 44	Eliab	Page 32, 34, 36
Ammihud -[Ephraim tribe]	page 24	Bela -king	Page 14	Eliasaph -son of Lael [Levi tribe]	Page 27
Ammihud -[Naphtali tribe]	Page 50	Ben Oni -Benjaman	Page 15, 19, 44	Eliasaph -son of Reuel [Gad tribe]	Page 23, 34
Ammihud -[Simeon tribe]	Page 50	Benammi	Page 7	Elidad	Page 50
Amminadab	Page 21, 23	Benjaman -Ben Oni	Page 15, 19, 44	Elieazer -priest	Page 50
Ammishaddai	Page 25	Beor -father of king Bela	Page 14	Eliezer -servant of Abraham	Page 8
Amor-ite	Page 5	Beor -father of Balaam	Page 33	Eliezer -son of Moses	Page 21
Amram	Page 16, 21, 27	Beriah	Page 18, 46	Eliphaz	Page 11
Amraphel -king	Page 9	Bethuel	Page 7	Elishama -son of Ammihud	Page 24, 34
Anah -daughter of Zibeon a Hivite	Page 11	Bezalel	Page 22	Elishan	Page 4
Anah -nephew of Duke Anah	Page 13	Bilhah -handmaiden	Page 15	Elisheba -daughter	Page 21
Anah -son & Duke of Seir a Horite	Page 13	Bilhan	Page 13	Elizaphan	Page 27, 34, 50
Anak	Page 31	Birsha -king	Page 9	Elizur	Page 23, 34
Anamim	Page 4	Bukki	Page 50	Elkanah	Page 21
Arad -king	Page 33	Buz	Page 7	Elon -Hittite	Page 11
Aram	Page 6-7	Cain	Page 3	Elon -son of Zebulun	Page 17, 41

Elzaphan	Page 21	Haran	Page 7	Japheth	Page 4
Enan	Page 25	Hararmaueth	Page 6	Jared	Page 3
Enoch	Page 3	Havilah	Page 4, 6	Jashub	Page 40
Enosh	Page 3	Hazo	Page 7	Javan	Page 4
Ephah	Page 8	Heber	Page 18, 46	Jeaer	Page 19
Epher	Page 8	Hebron	Page 16, 21, 27	Jebus-ite	Page 5
Ephod	Page 50	Helek	Page 42	Jeezer	Page 42
Ephraim	Page 15, 18, 24, 43	Helon	Page 24	Jehleel	Page 17
Er	Page 15, 17, 39	Hemam	Page 13	Jemuel -son of Simeon (Nemuel)	Page 16
Eran	Page 43	Hemdan	Page 13	Jephunneh	Page 29, 50
Eri	Page 18, 38	Hepher	Page 42	Jerah	Page 6
Esau	Page 11	Heth	Page 5	Jeshurn	Page 53
Eshban	Page 13	Hezron -son of Perez	Page 15, 17, 39	Jesui -son of Asher (Isui)	Page 46
Eve	Page 3	Hezron -son of Reuben	Page 16, 36,	Jethro -(Reul)	Page 21
Ezbun	Page 18	Hiv-ite	Page 5	Jetur	Page 8
Ezbun	Page 38	Hoglah -daughter	Page 42	Jeush -Duke	Page 11
Ezer -Duke	Page 13	Hori	Page 13, 29	Jezer -son of Naphtali	Page 19, 47
Gad	Page 15, 18, 38	Hul	Page 6	Jidlaph	Page 7
Gaddi	Page 30	Hupham -son of Benjamin	Page 44	Jimna -son of Asher (Jimnah)	page 46
Gaddiel	Page 30	Huppim -son of Benjamin	Page 19	Jimnah -son of Asher (Jimna)	Page 18
Gaham	Page 7	Hur -[Judah tribe]	Page 21-22	Job -son of Issachar	Page 17
Gamaliel	Page 24, 34	Hushim -son of Dan	Page 19	Jobab	Page 6
Gatam -Duke	Page 11	Hushram -king	Page 14	Jobabo -king	Page 14
Gemalli	Page 30	Huz	Page 7	Jochebed -daughter & wife	Page 16, 21
Gera	Page 19	Igal	Page 29	Jogli	Page 50
Gershom	Page 21	Irad	Page 3	Jokshan	Page 8
Gershon	Page 16, 27	Isaac	Page 8, 11	Joktan	Page 6
Gether	Page 6	Iscah -daughter	Page 7	Jopheth	Page 3
Geuel	Page 30	Ishbak	Page 8	Joseph -[Issachar tribe]	Page 29
Gideoni	Page 24	Ishmael	Page 8	Joseph -son Jacob	Page 15, 18
Gilead	Page 42	Ishuah -son of Asher	Page 18	Joshua	Page 50
Girgash-ite	Page 5	Issachar	Page 15, 17, 40	Jubal	Page 3
Gomer	Page 4	Isui -son of Asher (Jesui)	Page 18	Judah	Page 15, 17, 39
Guni	Page 19, 47	Ithamar	Page 21	Judith -daughter	Page 11
Hadad	Page 8	Ithran	Page 13	Judith -wife	Page 11
Hadad -king	Page 14	Izehar -(Izhar)	Page 27	Kahath	Page 27
Hadoram	Page 6	Izhar -(Izehar)	Page 16, 21	Kedemah	Page 8
Hagar -handmaiden	Page 8	Jaalam -Duke	Page 11	Kemuel	Page 7, 50
Haggi	Page 18, 38	Jabal	Page 3	Kenan	Page 3
Ham	Page 3-4	Jachin	Page 16, 37	Kenaz -Duke	Page 11
Hamath-ite	Page 5	Jacob	Page 11, 15	Kesed or Chesed	Page 7
Hamor -Hivite	Page 15	Jahleel	Page 41	Ketura -concubine	Page 8
Hamul	Page 15, 17, 39	Jahzeel	Page 19, 47	Keydar	Page 8
Hanniel	Page 50	Jair	Page 49	Kittim	Page 4
Hanoch	Page 8, 16, 36	Jamin	Page 16, 37	Kohath	Page 16, 21

Korah -[Levite tribe]	Page 32	Methusael	Page 3	Oholiab	Page 22
Korah -Duke, son of Esau	Page 11	Methuselah	Page 3	Omar -Duke	Page 11
Korah -son of Izhar	Page 21	Mibsam	Page 8	On	Page 32
Laban	Page 7	Micheal	Page 30	Onam	Page 13
Lael	Page 27	Midian	Page 8	Onan	Page 15, 17, 39
Lamech	Page 3	Milcah -daughter of Haran, wife	Page 7	Ophir	Page 6
Leah -daughter	Page 7	Milcah -daughter of Zelophehad	Page 42	Oshea -son of Nun (Joshua)	Page 29
Leah -wife	Page 15	Miriam -daughter	Page 21	Ozni -son of Gad	Page 38
Lehabim	Page 4	Mishael	Page 21	Pallu	Page 16, 36
Letushim	Page 8	Mishma	Page 8	Palti	Page 29
Leummim	Page 8	Mizraim	Page 4	Paltiel	Page 50
Levi	Page 15, 16, 27	Mizzah -Duke	Page 11	Pamach	Page 50
Lezer	Page 42	Moab	Page 7	Pathrusim	Page 4
Libni	Page 16, 27	Molech	Page 33	Pedahel -son of Ammihud	Page 50
Lot	Page 7	Moses	Page 21, 32-34	Pedahzur	Page 24
Lotan -Duke	Page 13	Muppim -son of Benjamin	Page 19	Pegiel	Page 25, 34
Lud	Page 6	Mushi	Page 16	Peleg	Page 6, 7
Ludim	Page 4	Mushi	Page 16, 27	Peleth	Page 32
Maacah	Page 7	Naamah -daughter	Page 3	Pharez	Page 15, 17, 39
Machi -father	Page 30	Naaman	Page 19	Phicol	Page 53
Machir	Page 15, 42	Naaman -son of Bela	Page 44	Phinehas	Page 21, 33
Machir	Page 49	Nadab	Page 21	Phut	Page 4
Madai	Page 4	Nahath -Duke	Page 11	Phuvah -son of Issachar (Pua)(h)	Page 17
Magog	Page 4	Nahbi	Page 30	Pildash	Page 7
Mahalaleel	Page 3	Nahor -the grandfather	Page 7	Potiphera	Page 15
Mahalath -daughter	Page 8	Nahor -the grandson	Page 7	Pua(h) -son of Issachar (Phuvah)	Page 40
Mahalath -wife	Page 11	Nahshon -son of Amminadab	Page 34	Puah -midwife	Page 20
Mahali	Page 16	Naphish	Page 8	Putiel	Page 21
Mahlah -daughter	Page 42	Naphtali	Page 15, 19, 47	Raamah	Page 4
Mahli	Page 16, 27	Naphtuhim	Page 4	Rachel -daughter, wife	Page 7, 15
Maikiel -son of Asher (Malchiel)	Page 18	Nebaioth -Nebajoth	Page 8	Raphu	Page 29
Malchiel -son of Asher (Maikiel)	Page 46	Nebajoth - Nebaioth	Page 8	Rebekah -daughter, wife	Page 7, 11
Manahath	Page 13	Nemuel -son of Eliab	Page 32, 36	Reu	Page 7
Manasseh	Page 18, 24, 42	Nemuel -son of Simeon (Jemuel)	Page 37	Reuben	Page 15, 16, 36
Mashech	Page 4	Nepheg	Page 21	Reuel -(Jethro)	Page 11, 21
Massa	Page 8	Nethaneel	Page 24, 34	Reumah	Page 7
Matred -mother	Page 14	Nimrod	Page 4	Riphath	Page 4
Me Zahab	Page 14	Noah	Page 3	Rosh	Page 19
Mechizedec	Page 9	Noah -daughter of Zelophehad	Page 42	Sabtah	Page 4
Medad	Page 28	Nun	Page 29	Salah	Page 6
Medan	Page 8	Obal	Page 6	Salu -prince	Page 33
Mehetabel -daughter	Page 14	Ocran	Page 25	Samlah -king	Page 14
Mehujael	Page 3	Og -king	Page 33, 49	Sarah -wife	Page 8
Merari	Page 16, 27	Ohad	Page 16	Seba	Page 4
Mesh	Page 6	Ohan	Page 37	Seir	Page 13

Serah -daughter of Asher	Page 18, 46
Sered	Page 17, 41
Serug	Page 7
Seth	Page 3
Sethur	Page 30
Shammah -Duke	Page 11
Shammua	Page 29
Shaphat	Page 29
Shaul	Page 16, 37
Shaul -king	Page 14
Sheba	Page 4, 6, 8
Shechem -son of Gilead	Page 42
Shechem -son of Hamor a Hivite	Page 15
Shedeur	Page 23
Shelah	Page 15, 17, 39
Sheleph	Page 6
Shelomi	Page 50
Shelumiel	Page 23, 34
Shem	Page 3, 6
Shemember	Page 9
Shemida	Page 42
Shemuel	Page 50
Shepho	Page 13
Sheshai	Page 31
Shillem	Page 19, 47
Shimei -son of Gershon (Shimi)	Page 27
Shimi - son of Gershon (Shimei)	Page 16
Shimron	Page 40
Shinab -king	Page 9
Shiphrah -midwife	Page 20
Shiphtan	Page 50
Shobal -Duke	Page 13
Shua	Page 15
Shuah	Page 8
Shuham	Page 45
Shuni	Page 18, 38
Shupham	Page 44
Shuthelah	Page 43
Sidon	Page 5
Sihon -King	Page 33, 49
Simeon	Page 15-16, 37
Sin-ite	Page 5
Sodi	Page 30
Subtecha	Page 4
Susi	Page 30
Tabah	Page 7
Tahan	Page 43
Talmai	Page 31
Tamar -daughter	Page 15
Tarshish	Page 4
Tema	Page 8
Teman -Duke	Page 11
Terah	Page 7
Thahash	Page 7
Tidal -king	Page 9
Timna -Daughter	Page 13
Timna -wife	Page 11
Tiras	Page 4
Tirzah -daughter	Page 42
Togarmah	Page 4
Tola	Page 40
Tubal Cain -son of Lamech	Page 3
Tubal -son of Japheth	Page 4
Unknown daughter older -Lot	Page 7
Unknown daughter -Shua	Page 15
Unknown daughter younger -Lot	Page 7
Unknown wife -Judah	Page 15
Unknown wife -Lot	Page 7
Unknown wife -Putiel	Page 21
Unknown wife -Simeon	Page 16, 37
Uri	Page 22
Uz	Page 6, 13
Uzah	Page 6
Uzziel	Page 16, 21, 27
Vophsi	Page 30
Zaavan	Page 13
Zaccur	Page 29
Zebulun	Page 15, 17, 41
Zelophehad	Page 42
Zemaz-ite	Page 5
Zepho -Duke	Page 11
Zephon -son of Gad (Ziphion)	Page 38
Zerah	Page 15, 17, 39
Zerah -Duke	Page 11
Zerah -father of king Jobab	Page 14
Zerah -son of Simeon (Zohar)	Page 37
Zibeon -Hivite	Page 11
Zibeon -Horite Duke	Page 13
Zichri	Page 21
Zillah -wife	Page 3
Zilpah -handmaiden	Page 15
Zimran	Page 8
Zimri	Page 33
Ziphion -son of Gad (Zephon)	Page 18
Zippor	Page 33
Zipporah -wife	Page 21
Zithri	Page 21
Zohar -son of Simeon (Zerah)	Page 16
Zuar	Page 24
Zur -leader	Page 33
Zuriel	Page 27, 34
Zurishaddai	Page 23

68

Sincere thanks to:
BibleGateway.com
Bible History on Line
Biblos.com
Jewishvirtuallibrary.org

Resource materials:

Amplified Bible
Contemporary English Version Bible
King James Version Bible
New King James Version Bible
New International Version Bible
The Voice Bible

Special thanks to:

Biblegateway.com
and
Author, Stephen Caesar

To contact the author:
tmccullough8250@gmail.com

www.ingramcontent.com/pod-product-compliance
Lightning Source LLC
Chambersburg PA
CBHW041818080526

44587CB00004B/136